# A
# PLACE CALLED
# THROUGH

JACKIE LISTEN

# Praise for *A Place Called Through*

*A Place Called Through* will warm your soul and encourage you to follow the strong voice within you to press forward into your destiny. Jackie's story reminds us that our steps are ordered by God and that this exciting journey is rewarding and full when we pursue these steps wide open. You will be inspired as you read!

**Donald Sherman**
CEO - McClain Bank

～

I read that when a storm comes, cows will turn and try to outrun it. Buffaloes, on the other hand, turn and run "through" it. The difference is the cows spend longer in the storm than the buffaloes who run "through" it. The stories Jackie shares in this book will challenge you and encourage you to find the *"Place Called Through."* God has a way "through" the storm that will get where you need to be quicker than trying to outrun the storm.

**David Wright**
Co-Founder - M&MW Coaching and Consulting
Co-Pastor - Emerge International Church
Ziglar Legacy Coaching Head Coach

～

Reading this book transported me back to the days when we slept with the front door open, keys in the pickup, and the smell of mom's peach cobbler cooling on the kitchen table. What a wonderful woven tapestry of love, faith, and family. *A Place Called Through* is truly a must read!

**Dr. Nathanial "Coach" Hearne**
Author of *FRIDAY NIGHT LIGHTS: THE UNTOLD STORIES BEHIND THE LIGHTS*

～

It has been my pleasure to know Jackie Listen for over 30 years in a friendship that has expanded our business, family, and faith. From cleaning pig pens, to praying over land no one wanted, to celebrating an incredible career at the bank, Jackie has always poured encouragement to those lucky enough to be around him. As one of the most hard-working men I have ever known, Jackie not only talks the talk, but he walks the walk. His down to earth, grass-roots message connects on a deep level with anyone going through a rough patch in life. His real-life stories demonstrate what faith and determination can get you through, all while making you laugh along the way.

In *A Place Called Through*, Jackie walks you through his life full of obstacles and opportunities. He shares his unique experiences, showing vulnerability and strength in equal parts. His ease of speech and southern drawl comes across in his writing which makes for an even more enjoyable read.

**Rick Newby**
District Manager - Farmers Insurance

~

Jackie Listen is one of the most "down-home" writers and communicators that possesses the incredible ability to take everyday life experiences and develop a life-changing teaching for those who will listen. His rise in life from obscurity to notoriety is one of the most powerful testimonies you will ever hear. Jackie is "the real deal" and so is his powerful book. I'm confident *A Place Called Through* will equip and prepare you to successfully pass through any present challenges to attain God's Plan and Purpose for your life!

**Terry Bates**
Lead Pastor - OKC Faith Church

~

*A Place Called Through* is a powerful and uplifting book that inspires people to believe in themselves and in the ultimate power of God. In this survival guide, Jackie Listen shares his own experiences of overcoming obstacles and challenges through faith and perseverance. The insights and practical advice provided in this book are not only valuable for those going through difficult times, but they are also applicable to everyday life situations. I highly recommend this book to anyone who needs encouragement and inspiration to keep going, no matter what life throws at them. It's a true reminder that with God by our side, all things are indeed possible.

**Michelle Prince**
Author, Speaker & CEO - Performance Publishing Group
Prince Performance Group, LLC

~

Every life has hills and valleys, and every life has **"A Place Called Through."** Jackie Listen is a great storyteller and shares what he calls the "Red Sea Moments" in his life...the times when God got him through the deepest, darkest spots. Jackie teaches us that quitting is not an option. Learning how to trust and move through the challenges of life are critical to succeeding. These are the words to live by from the guy who has lived it himself. This book is a real winner!

**Kevin Williams**
Guitarist, humorist, speaker
Gaither Vocal Band

∾

Truly there are not too many people on this planet that live a life to the fullest. One of those special people is Jackie Listen. His story is powerful and relatable to all generations realizing we have an entrepreneurial spirit within us. I truly enjoy Jackie's forward, authentic style of humble beginnings to create impact in so many people's lives and careers, especially mine. Overall, this book provides a glimpse into Jackie's family history and the values that shaped their upbringing. It highlights the resilience and resourcefulness of their ancestors, who built good names for themselves and exemplified the "Oklahoma Standard" through their acts of service, honor, and kindness. Jackie emphasizes the importance of hard work, perseverance, and faith in shaping his character and preparing him for adulthood. Living a legacy is what it's all about, and I assure you that you will be inspired to have a legacy after reading this book.

**Steven VanCauwenberg**
Author, Real Estate Investor & Entrepreneur
Founder of Savvy Brand
Podcast host of The Savvy Radio Show

∾

I have known Jackie Listen for 31 years as a personal friend, banker, and business coach. He is one of the most sincere, God-fearing men I know. His life has been full of obstacles, perseverance, and great successes. His success is a testament of God's presence and his using Jackie as an example and instrument for others to watch, listen and learn from. As a wise old man once said, "Listen to those in whom have *earned the right* to be listened to". Jackie Listen has.

**Rob Roberts**
Entrepreneur & Real Estate Investor

∾

*A Place Called Through* is never easy, but GOD can make it simple. The trials and troubles Jackie faced could not have been overcome by him or man alone. Jackie endured, had faith, and with GOD's help, was led through the valleys and up and down the hills. It wasn't until last year that I became a reader, and that's because of Jackie's coaching. I have been so inspired and encouraged from this book that I want to prepare myself to write a book one day. I am forever grateful for the imprint and impact that Jackie has had on my family's life.

**Rayson Sanchez**
CEO - Providence Construction & Restorations Company, LLC

What a gift of inspiration and demonstration of God's faithfulness through the ups and downs of life! Jackie's storytelling draws you in and reminds you that God still performs 'Red Sea miracles' today, and you can trust Him. It's my privilege to know Jackie Listen. He is a great man of God.

**Wes Jackson**
Executive Director/Pastor - New Hope Farms, Inc

# Foreword by Tom Ziglar

I have a question for you. Are you thirsty? I remember as a child playing outside in the hot 105 degree Texas heat. I would get so thirsty that I would find a garden hose wherever I was to get a drink. First I had to let the water run for 30 seconds or so to clear the hose "taste" and get the hot water out of it. Then I would start to drink the cool water. I can taste it now! After a minute or two I would then run the water over my head, and if a friend was nearby I would give them a good spray!

Did that story make you thirsty? More likely you are experiencing a different kind of thirst. Is your soul thirsty? Do you feel like the last few years you have been exposed to a searing hot desert wind and no matter what you do you still feel parched, dried-up, and shriveled? You need water, and not the type of water that comes from a garden hose.

This book is a cool pitcher of water for your soul. You will find yourself immersed in story after story of life lessons that refresh, cleanse, and help you make sense out of the journey you are on. You will begin to find the deeper meaning in the Zig Ziglar quote "It's not what happens to you that determines how far you will go in life; it is how you handle what happens to you."

If you are ready to happen to life instead of life happening to you then I encourage you to do two things. Start with reading this book. Drink deeply and know that better days are ahead and what you have been through is preparing you for something meaningful. Next, reach out to Jackie. Every time I talk to Jackie, I leave the conversation encouraged and more hopeful than before. The water is ready - start drinking!

**Tom Ziglar**
CEO - Zig Ziglar Corporation

# CONTENTS

# STRETCHED

"We all experience times of testing, which is normal for
every human being. But God will be faithful to you.
He will screen and filter the severity, nature, and timing
of every test or trial you face so that you can bear it.
And each test is an opportunity to trust him more, for
along every trial God has provided for you a way of
escape that will bring you out of it victoriously."
1 Corinthians 10:13, TPT

**I WAS HONORED TO BE** in Class IX of the Oklahoma Agricultural Leadership Program from 1998-2000. Our instructor and mentor, Dr. Bob Terry, told us in our very first meeting, "As leaders, my job is to 'stretch your box.' But here's the good news: once your box is stretched, it never goes back."

"God knows a good stretch in life will lead us to our purpose."
Jackie Listen

My good friend Gene Cobb recently sent me this quote: "One day you will tell your story of how you've overcome what you're going through now, and it will become part of someone else's survival guide."

I've also adopted this quote for my life: "Blessed are the flexible, for with God's help, they shall not be bent out of shape!"

This is a true story about how God will lead you through any difficulty life throws at you—so long as you believe and trust in Him. I dedicate this book to my loving wife of 41 years, Paula, who has been right there by my side through it all. Her encouragement, toughness, wisdom, and loving heart have always encouraged me to be my best! I also want to dedicate this book to my children, my son-in-law, and, as of this writing, my first grandson, who sparks joy every day!

I also dedicate this book to all those who have touched my life in some way. There are so many of you. To each of you, I am forever grateful!

The purpose of this book is to show my kids, grandkids, and future great-grandchildren that all things are possible with and through God. My hope also is that this book will be a survival guide for those who need encouragement and inspiration to persevere!

## FROM THE PIG PEN TO THE INK PEN

One day, I was telling my little brother Bobby about writing this book. He told me I should name it "From the Pig Pen to the Ink Pen." I thought to myself, *Yeah, you're right. That's how my life has gone.*

# INTRODUCTION

IN 2014, I MET A man named Steven VanCauwenbergh through a string of connections. We were introduced by Robert Elder, whom I'd met through my friend Rob Roberts. These men are successful real estate investors in Oklahoma City. This was back during my banking days, when I helped them with loans for their investments.

The day I met Steven, he came into my office in Noble, Oklahoma, and said, "I just drove past at least 30 banks from Oklahoma City to Noble. What am I doing here?" I laughed and said, "Partner, you're getting ready to find out." He laughed too! We spent two hours at that first meeting, and Steven shared his amazing story with me about the first investment home he bought. He also gave me two books he had written about rental properties. After that, I started telling him about what I'd begun calling the "1980s Red Sea miracles."

"You need to write these down," he said.

"I don't know anything about that!" I said. Truthfully, I hadn't considered myself much of a writer at the time.

"Man, do it for your kids and family," he said.

"You got me there!" I responded.

That was the day I first considered writing down the stories in this book. And now, you're either holding my book in your hands or hearing me on Audible. I'm grateful that God sent Steven to encourage me to do this. My hope is that my kids, grandkids, and great grandkids will learn from the hard lessons my family and I went through. This is a faith-based book about a young entrepreneur's family, and their in-laws, who had everything that could go wrong, go wrong—and how God brought them through their trials one miracle at a time. So, thank you Steven for encouraging me to do this. Ever since that day, I've told myself, "I'm going to write these stories down in a book for my family." I started it several times but could never get my feet off the ground. I "re-fired" out of banking in December of 2019, and the following year I became a Ziglar certified coach. When our coaching group was encouraged to bring things back that we wanted to work on in 2021, God put a message in my heart: "It's time for the book."

Back in 2013, my wife and I had the opportunity to go for a three-day "Born to Win" seminar at the Ziglar Corporation. It was phenomenal. After one of the sessions, Paula and I had the opportunity to speak with Julie Ziglar, the daughter of "Zig" Ziglar. Julie edited many of her father's books. We told Julie we thought our daughter possessed the talent to write books, and she suggested we speak to Michelle Prince, whose contact information she'd provided me with.

In January 2021, I'd mentioned my goals to the Ziglar coaches about writing my book. I prayed, "God, if I'm to use Michelle Prince as my publisher, let it come through Tom Ziglar." The very next week, I received an email from Tom saying: "Jackie, I don't know if you've ever heard of Michelle Prince, but here's her contact information. She's having a Book Bound webinar this week." That was my confirmation. I signed up, and that's how this book finally came to pass. (When I spoke to Michelle sometime later and told her I'd been wanting to write this book for seven years, she said, "Jackie it just wasn't time until now.")

My prayer for this book is to inspire and encourage those who might find themselves right in the middle of a storm they did not ask for. Hopefully these stories will show faith, hope, forgiveness, trust in God, and that quitting is never an option. Throughout my life, a lot of things did not go as I thought they would. There were many days of prayer, tears, and enormous pressure. But at the end of the day, Jesus was always there. As I'm looking back writing these stories, I see God's plan at work.

When I was a kid, there was an amusement park in Northeast Oklahoma City called Springlake. Many of us baby boomers, and the generation above us, have fond memories of this park. There is a Metro Technology Center facility there now, and there are pictures on the walls of a time gone by. At the park was a huge rollercoaster called the Big Dipper, which was built in 1929. I vividly remember climbing that first big slope. The fall from the top of that first hill was exhilarating!

The stories ahead are a little like that rollercoaster. So, tighten your seatbelt—here we go!

# MY BEGINNINGS

"Your calling is not meant to fit who you are
today, but who God created you to be."
Tom Ziglar

"For who hath despised the day of small things."
Zechariah 4:10

"Success is the sum of small efforts,
repeated day in and day out."
Robert Collier

**MY ROOTS RUN DEEP IN** Oklahoma. My family consisted mainly of farmers and schoolteachers. In 1916, my great-grandparents on my mom's side, CM and Mary Jane Thomas, moved their family from Cumberland, Oklahoma to a 160-acre farm in Jones, Oklahoma. My other great-grandparents on her side, W.E. & Bessie Mae Lewis, farmed 160 acres in Jones. Both of my mother's grandparents—the Lewises and Thomases—helped build and establish a church in their area, which is still there today.

My great-grandparents on my dad's side, McGannon and Mollie P. Barnes, settled on another 160-acre farm right after the land rush in Jones. And in the 1890s, my other great-grandparents on my dad's side, Otto and Minnie Listen, immigrated from Germany and eventually settled on a 320-acre sheep farm in Edmond, Oklahoma. They all farmed, helped their communities, and built good names for themselves. They exemplified what we call the "Oklahoma Standard," which is a statewide initiative preserving and promoting a culture of caring citizens by encouraging Acts of Service, Honor, and Kindness.

For the first seven years of my life, we lived with my Grandma Zetta Ione Listen on her 80-acre farm at Britton and Post Road, just west of my hometown of Jones. Grandma Listen had a great impact on my life. She lost her husband, my Grandpa Herbert Listen, in 1934 at the age of 35 from a ruptured appendix. She was left raising five children, while also managing debt on the farm in the middle of the Great Depression.

Grandma had her teaching certificate, and she taught school to put food on the table. She would tell me stories of growing up in the horse and buggy days as a little pioneer girl here in Oklahoma. She also remembered all her students. When she saw one of their names in the paper, she would tell me what type of student they'd been. She taught phonics in the first grade and was a great teacher.

My dad, Robert "Bob" Listen, was her youngest boy. Dad had an eye for livestock, and he started his small Poland China Hog herd and dairy with five dairy cows after graduating from high school. Dad dated my mother, Betty Thomas, and told her he couldn't get married until he had a good peanut crop. Unfortunately for Mom, that took seven years! My brother Bart is the oldest boy, I'm the middle child (three years younger), and my brother Bobby is six years younger than me.

Jackie (bottom left) with his older brother Bart (top left), Mother Betty, Father Bob and younger brother Bobby (sitting in Bob's lap)

My first seven years on Grandma's farm were precious in many ways. My cousin Stevie lived on the farm just up the hill from Grandma's house. His mom is my Aunt Marjorie Millican—Dad's oldest sister— and her husband is my Uncle Cecil. They had a huge positive impact on my life. Stevie is a year and a half older than me. We both have incredible memories of our daily adventures climbing trees, building forts in the hay barn, and getting Silver, our little Shetland pony, to buck both of us off in Grandma's front yard. Life was simple and full of fun. Stevie and I still talk about how much fun we had and how we remember all the innocent trouble we got into.

In 1968, Mom and Dad built a new brick home on 80 acres, just one mile north of Grandma Listen's farm. We moved our hog and beef cattle operation there, and our dairy farm stayed at Grandma Listen's.

When we moved, I went to work carrying water buckets to the pigs. Dad paid us with our pick of six pigs per year. We had some of the best to pick from in the nation. We would show the pigs at the local, county, and state fairs. Dad provided the feed and let us keep all the proceeds. This was my first experience with the free enterprise system.

Jackie at a pig show as a young boy

We did our chores every morning, starting around 5:30. My mom was very kind in the mornings. She would come in and say, "Jackie, it's time to get up!" Bart and I would get up and go brave the elements to feed and water the pigs. Bobby was too young at the time for chores. Although the farm operation was different by the time he was old enough to work on it, it was still tough, and he has plenty of his own stories he can tell.

Bart and I had our separate designated chores. It didn't matter what the weather was like—whether sweltering hot or freezing cold, chores still had to be done. I like to say this was a valuable learning experience that a lot of children don't get the opportunity to have. I'm very grateful for the work ethic instilled in me at such a young age. Looking back, I see the valuable lessons that have served me well in my adult years. I'll admit, there were times I didn't want to do chores! But Dad said, "If the animals don't eat, then you don't eat." I sure understood that!

My mom was great through it all, kindly encouraging me and my brothers on those frigid mornings. There is a special place in heaven for mothers who raise three ornery boys. My mom got up early, bottle fed baby calves, cooked our meals, and washed clothes all day long. Between our chore clothes, school clothes, and sports uniforms, there were mounds of laundry—especially with a livestock farm like ours. Mom wore many hats, and I'm forever grateful and blessed for her loving kindness and the timely wisdom she instilled in us. She was also faithful to have us in church every time the doors opened. Our mother is 88 years old as of this writing. She did a phenomenal job of caring and raising us three Listen boys. Thank you, Mom!

Mom's parents, Jackson Douglas and Eve Mae Thomas, lived three quarters of a mile west of our hog farm. PaPaw farmed all his life, and NaNaw helped him everywhere she could. They both were glowing examples in my young life. They were faithful to be in church twice on Sunday and every Wednesday evening. NaNaw was a juvenile diabetic, and she taught me how important it was for her to be on a strict diet and exercise program. I learned all about consistency from her at a young age. My grandparents helped me enjoy a happy childhood, and for that I'm forever grateful!

My entrepreneurial spirit developed at a young age. We received *Boy's Life Magazine*, a great source for a young boy in a country setting. One fond memory of mine is when I saw two knives advertised for sale in *Boy's Life* for $1.50. Right away, I knew I *had* to have them. I asked Mom about it, and she said, "You can buy them by writing a check." I told her I didn't know how. So, she had me get my checkbook out, and right there I wrote my first check in pencil for $1.50, payable to the Viking Knife Company. She also taught me what a stamp was and how to address an envelope. Off in the mail my check went, and I anxiously awaited my delivery at the mailbox every day.

One day, they finally came. Excitement overcame me. They were two very small knives, but to a nine-year-old boy like me, they were grand! Also, when my bank statement came in the next month, Mom sat me down and taught me how to balance my checkbook—another valuable lesson I learned at a young age!

I got my real education in a dairy barn in Jones. Of my brothers, I was the accident-prone one, so I learned about resilience at an early age. One Saturday morning, my cousin Stevie and I were milking cows. Dad had warned me that the way I was opening the door would allow too many cows to come in at the same time, so I had better pay attention. Well, when you're a young teenage boy, there's a problem with your attention span. The first cows are what I call the "pros"—they're anxious to get in the barn. They know they are going to have a great grain meal and be milked, which relieves the stress on their utter. Anyway, I wasn't paying attention as two cows tried to push through. They squeezed me right out the door. My arm got jammed, and there was a 16-penny nail that caught me on the hind end. After managing my way off the door, I didn't know what was hurting worse, my hind end or my arm. Stevie was laughing at first because I was running around in circles holding my arm and hind end. When he saw I was hurt, he took me up to Grandma Listen's house. Dad was there eating breakfast with Grandma. He asked,

"What's wrong?" and I said, "I think I broke my arm!" He thought I had just sprained it, but Grandma said, "No, he needs to be looked at."

The nurse at the hospital was a little rough X-raying my arm. She thought it was just sprained, but when they looked at the X-ray it showed it was broken. She said, "Well, your arm's broke!" I said, "I've been trying to tell everyone that for two hours!"

On went the cast, which was extremely inconvenient. But on the way home, I realized the lone bright spot was that I'd get out of doing chores for a while. I said, "Dad, I'm sorry I broke my arm, because it looks like I'll be out of commission for a while to do chores." Here's where resilience kicks in. Dad said, "There's nothing wrong with your other arm. You can't milk, but you can water hogs." I thought, *Man, even a broken arm can't get me out of chores!*

One thing about my dad: He was tough on his boys, but in a good way. Isn't life like that? As I'd said previously, my grandpa Herbert—Dad's dad—died when Dad was only two years old. Dad grew up not having a dad in his life. When he was older, he told me that Bart and I knew more about business at 15 than he had at 30. The dairy barn was a key part in my upbringing. It prepared me for what was to come.

I've always loved horses. One day my dad mentioned that if I wanted to learn more about horses, I should go over to Donnie and Linda Jones's place. They were our neighbors to the south. I contacted them, and they were happy to let me come and learn from them. They had a pretty place with a nice barn, pasture, and an arena. For a couple of years, I went to their place most evenings, and they taught me all there was to know about horses. Donnie and Linda had an immense impact on my life. I won't ever forget all the helpful lessons I learned from these two selfless individuals and friends.

The rest of my adolescent years consisted mainly of typical teenager things. Football, girlfriends, heartbreaks, farm work, hauling hay, and my first paying job sacking groceries. Winning, losing, learning, and dreaming. Through it all, I remained determined to own my own business one day.

The last semester of my sophomore year, a spokesperson for Foster Estes Vo-Tech came by my school. (I've always loved cars.) In those days, you had to apply and compete if there was more than one student applying to a program. I applied for the autobody course, and I learned another student had applied as well. But I was fortunate enough to win the position, which turned out to be a steppingstone in my future.

# TURNING POINT: THE START OF MY CAREER

**Turning Point: a time at which a decisive change in a situation occurs, especially one with beneficial results.**
**Oxford Language Dictionary**

*"Now may the God of hope fill you with all joy and peace as you believe in him, so that you may abound in hope by the power of the Holy Spirit."*
Romans 15:13

**I'LL NEVER FORGET MY FIRST** day of vo-tech with my instructor, Steve Prieto. I'd started wearing cowboy boots at the beginning of my sophomore year. And of course, all the guys had long feathered hair. This was the '70s, after all!

Mr. Prieto was asking different students random questions. He looked at me, the only one with cowboy boots on in the room, and said, "Listen, are you a goat roper?"

"No, sir. I'm a pig farmer!" I said.

The whole room burst out in laughter! Little did I know how valuable and impactful this experience would have on me and my future. One day, towards the end of my first year at vo-tech, Mr. Prieto said, "Listen, go apply at Bob Moore Cadillac in downtown Oklahoma City. They're looking for a part-time body shop helper." My Uncle, Gene Lassiter, was a car salesman there. I filled out my application, and when I dropped it off, I went by and asked my uncle if he would put in a good word for me. He said sure, then I waited to hear back.

Meanwhile, I'd sold a pig to Mr. Prieto, and it was time for him to come pick it up and take it to the butcher. He asked me if I ever heard back from Bob Moore Cadillac, and I told him I hadn't. Then he told me that Crossroad Chrysler Plymouth was hiring, and to give them a call.

The next day was a Friday. I called the body shop manager, applied, and he hired me on the spot for $3.00 an hour. I was to report to work on Monday with the few tools I had. But when I got home that afternoon, I got a call from Pat, the body shop manager at Bob Moore. "Jack, we've got your stall all ready," he said. "We need you to start work on Monday."

"Pat, I just took a job at Crossroads Chrysler Plymouth," I told him.

He said, "What are they paying you?"

"$3.00 per hour."

"Okay, how's $3.25 sound?" he said.

"You've got a deal!" I exclaimed.

I called the body shop manager at Crossroad Chrysler Plymouth and told him I was sorry, but I had gotten a better offer. Landing that job in the summer of 1978 was a turning point for me in many ways. I learned so much, had a ton of fun working, and prepared myself for the journey still to come. After graduating high school in 1979, I went on to take a full-time job at Bob Moore Cadillac.

# THE REAL ESTATE COWBOY

*"Whoever renders service to many puts himself in
line for greatness—great wealth, great return, great
satisfaction, great reputation, and great joy."*
Jim Rohn

**DAD BECAME A REALTOR IN** his late 40s, around 1977. He specialized in farmland and commercial properties. In 1980, he sold 160 acres to a retired professional rodeo cowboy by the name of Paul Howard. Paul had just started in the land development business. He had recently sold out one 160-acre tract in Nicoma Park, Oklahoma, and now he was interested in the area around Jones. I remember coming over to Dad's house after work and hearing him talk about meeting Paul. He explained Paul's business plan to me, so I had some knowledge of what he was doing. That same year, Bart had moved back from Cope, South Carolina, where he'd been managing a large purebred hog operation. Now he needed a job. Paul's business was growing, so he hired my brother.

Bart started making good money. He would tell me about the land and how much he was making, and *man*, it got me excited for him. One night, I had a vivid dream where I saw myself selling land.

The oil industry was booming, and Paul's land business was flourishing as well. One weekend, Paul's other salesman, Steve Jones, had gone on vacation. They needed help. Bart mentioned me, and Paul said to come on down. They had a lot of appointments that weekend. Paul briefly explained his process, and Bart had already been telling me how things operated there.

Guess what? I sold 20 acres that weekend and made more money than I'd made all month from pounding on fenders at the body shop.

Paul recognized my potential, and he went to work checking me out. He called my body shop manager, Eddie Rule, who gave me a good review. Eddie Rule had a great influence on my life and was a key mentor for me. He saw potential in me, and I saw a leader with character and integrity in him. Just recently, my cousin Rob Lassiter and I went to lunch with Eddie. (Rob is a few years younger than I am, and he also worked with Eddie after I left the body shop.) We both told Eddie the impact he'd had on our lives. If there's someone who has helped you in the past, and they are still alive, I highly recommend you tell them in person that you wouldn't be who you are today without their impact.

Paul was satisfied with Eddie's recommendation, so he offered me a full-time job selling land for him.

## REAL ESTATE

The oil industry in Oklahoma was booming due to the American hostages being held in Iran, the Iran oil embargo, oil shortages, and inflation. Oklahoma was and *is* an oil state. We had well-paying oil field jobs while the rest of the country was closing businesses left and right. General Motors' manufacturing plants were starting to lay workers off, and they ended up closing several plants. People needed to move to areas where they could find jobs—Oklahoma was one of those places.

At one point in 1981, there were 2,900 people moving to the state of Oklahoma every *week*. Due to the recession in other parts of the United States, people were pouring into our state, and they needed to secure quick housing. Paul Howard would buy 80-160 acres of land from a farmer who wanted to sell, and he would then develop and divide it into 1.5-to-5-acre tracts. He would sell the lots for a fair price with a down payment. He would carry the mortgage himself, and the property owners would pay him for the balance of the loan over a period of 10-20 years. We allowed mobile homes in our developments, so people were able to lock in their land payment at a better price (or at least equal to what they were paying for rent in a mobile home park or apartment). Besides the influx of people coming into the state, there were also people here who were tired of living in the city. Country living appealed to them.

Paul hired me in February of 1981, and I gave my two weeks' notice at Bob Moore Cadillac. Just like that, my new adventure began. Little did I know at that point the impact my new mentor would have on me.

Paul was a retired professional rodeo cowboy with only a third-grade education. But he knew more than most books could teach. He had lived quite an interesting life—from growing up as one of 12 siblings in Texas and traveling across states in a covered wagon and on horseback during the 1950s, to picking cotton, learning trades, and riding bareback horses on the professional rodeo circuit. His life truly could have been a movie! At one point, he even starred in a commercial for Ivory Snow soap, which you can find online at the following link: https://youtu.be/NPvuWuaWc1I.
(P&G - Ivory Snow - The Cowboy Twins - Vintage Commercial - 1960s - 1970s)

Paul riding bareback in 1968
at the Houston Astrodome

After retiring from rodeo, Paul made a living trading, selling cars and jewelry. He's one of the greatest salesmen I've ever known. One of the reasons he was such a great salesman was that he *always* told the customer the truth. He taught us that it was okay to tell the customer, "I don't know, but I will find the answer for you." That was an invaluable lesson for me.

Paul grew up in a family of six boys and six girls. "We fought!" he often said. When he hired me, he told me that my brother Bart had started working for him first, so if we ever got into a fight or argument, I would be the first to go. I totally understood—but I also told him that wouldn't be an issue. I was so excited—after my short weekend stint with Paul, I'd already grown to love selling land. We were providing a way for people to build wealth and get out of paying rent by owning their own property.

The training began with learning how to get people to come out and see if we had land they liked. We ran little reader ads in the newspaper under the "acreages for sale" section. Potential customers would call, and we had a system that worked very well. I was pretty nervous the first call I took. The gentlemen on the other end of the phone "hardly had a chance to come up for air" as they say. And of course, I couldn't land the appointment.

Paul overheard the conversation from his office. "Mr. Listen, come into my office," he said.

I thought, *Great, he's going to fire me right off the bat*. But Paul was a kind, great teacher. A good mentor knows that everybody makes mistakes along the way—the key is to keep trying until you get it right. Very kindly, he said to me, "Jackie, slow down. Let the person respond to your question." So, I did slow down. And almost immediately I started setting appointments and selling land.

Paul's patience with me brought to mind another lesson from my childhood: how important a great mentor/coach is in helping a young person to learn. I started playing baseball when I was seven, back when they called it peanuts. There was no t-ball back in those days;

it was kid pitch. Our coach was Delbert Taylor, and his son, Todd, was a good friend of mine. When my time came to learn to bat, Delbert explained the process of watching the bat hit the ball. But I kept striking out. For the life of me, I couldn't hit the ball.

Here's where a great coach kicks in—Delbert said, "Jackie, we're not leaving until you hit the ball." By that point I'd struck out 56 times, and I was thinking, *this is ridiculous*. But then, finally, the bat connected with the ball. I'd done it! Our team went undefeated that year. And to boot, I hit a couple of home runs.

*1969 Jones undefeated peanut champion team*

Just the other day, I saw my old coach and his wife. I thanked them for having a great impact on my life. I told Delbert he had all the qualities of a great coach. He never gave up on his players, and he instilled hope in them. And that's what Paul did for me that day in his office. Over time, he helped mold me into who I was to become.

The real estate acreage market was strong, very competitive, and we had some great salesmen as competition. If a customer didn't buy from us, then they usually bought from our competitor. With Paul's great sales method—what we called "good, clean selling"—we helped people work towards their dream of owning property. Business was booming, and we were growing.

Paul's oldest daughter, Paula, had been teaching at a Christian school. She decided she wanted to do something different, so Paul had her start coming to the office to type the paperwork for our closings. When I met Paula, I thought she liked Bart. Little did I know it was me she was interested in! So yes, I married the boss's daughter in August of 1981, and we are currently working on 42 years of marriage!

A quick, funny story here. One week before our wedding, Bart said to Paul, "I really need to talk to you." Paul had a policy that if an employee ever had an issue, we had to go to the office and nip it in the bud. So, Paul took Bart into his office and asked him what was wrong. Bart said, "Do you remember when Jackie first went to work for you, and you said if we got into a fight or argument that he would be the first to go?"

"Yes?" Paul said.

"I just want to know … if that happens today, does Jackie still go?" Bart said.

Paul burst out laughing. "Get out of my office!" he yelled.

Bart was laughing as well. Of course, he'd just been kidding around!

## THE WRECK

On October 4, 1981, our lives changed forever. On their way back from a church convention late one Sunday evening, my mother-in-law Alma Howard, my wife's baby brother Ty, my wife's grandmother Hazel, and my wife's great aunt Lucille and uncle Bud were all involved in a car wreck when a drunk woman ran a stop sign. We lost Hazel that night, and Ty and Uncle Bud the next day. Alma was seriously injured too—she spent over 45 days in the hospital—and Aunt Lucille required surgery. Thankfully, they both recovered. Paula and I had been married almost two months when this happened. At the age of 18, my wife had to plan the funeral for her grandmother and brother. Our entire family was devastated. My wife's sister, Tammy, was only 15. Both her and Paula lost their little brother, grandma, and great uncle.

Sometimes a tragedy causes a family to fall apart. But in our case, our family bonded together. We grew stronger. I saw my wife's grandfather, Lloyd Wilson, grow stronger in his faith. Paul and Alma's love for one another grew stronger as well. Alma survived the wreck and the ensuing trauma—a miracle in itself. She then worked hard to overcome her injuries, including having to learn to walk again. No matter what, she always kept pushing.

And I saw what real forgiveness looked like when Paul and Alma chose to forgive the drunk driver who'd caused the accident. Their faith was and is stronger than anything I ever could've imagined. A lot of lives were touched, and our family's faith was tested.

## MY FAITH MENTOR, WILSON

When I first met Paula's Grandpa, Lloyd Weldon Wilson (I came to call him "Wilson"), I was at his and Hazel's house to take my future wife out on a date. He was reading his Bible and I said, "Wilson, read me some scripture." He fired right back at me, "Read your own scripture!" That was the best thing he could have ever told me. After that, I started reading the Bible. From that point on—and especially later in my life—he had a huge impact on me. I spent the last 12 years of Wilson's life—every day—eating breakfast with him at 5:00 a.m. I learned so much about his life and the word of God during our breakfasts. When he passed in 2010, he was five months shy of 100. He was also still watering horses here on the ranch 60 days prior to his passing.

# THE FUN BEGINS

*"Celebrate life. After all, it's a very special occasion."*
Ken Blanchard

**IN NOVEMBER OF 1981, WE** closed on 160 acres of land, purchased from Walter and Yvonne Lopp. Walter and Yvonne went to school with my parents. My dad told me that Walter and his dad cleared the 160 acres by hand back when Walter was in high school. They also fenced the entire acreage with concrete posts, which they poured themselves. Some of the posts are still there today. After they farmed the property for a few years, Dad said they stopped because the land wasn't productive. By the time we bought the property, it was thick with small brushy oak trees. This was Paula and I's first land purchase in our names only (since there were no LLCs at that time). Later, this would turn into quite the issue.

I can vividly recall the $200,000 figure on the note we promised to pay back to the farmer. Keep in mind I was 20 years old at that point, and my wife was 18! Paul had just started in this business a year prior, and we were learning as we went. Paul and Bart were silent partners on this subdivision, which we named Sleepy Meadows Estates. If the property was zoned a certain way, then Oklahoma City would let you divide a larger piece into five-acre tracts where mobile homes were acceptable. I remembered this property from when I was a little boy, because the school bus I rode on went right by it every day. Although the property was in the Jones school district—which is where I attended all 12 years of my schooling—it was also in Oklahoma City city limits and was thereby subject to their bylaws and guidelines.

At that time, banks in Oklahoma didn't want to make loans on land. And when you were starting with nothing, leverage was the "name of the game." Our formula for buying the land was to offer a 10% down payment to the farmer. They would then finance the balance for 10 years at 10% interest. Next, we would go to a bank and borrow the money to develop the land, which consisted of surveying, platting, and building roads. The bank note would be put on a three to five-year payback period, usually at 16% interest. Lastly, when we sold a lot, we would finance our customers for up to 20 years at 12% interest. Our philosophy was that all the debt would be paid back in 10 years, and any receivable balance left gave us mailbox money.

Our contracts with the farmer allowed us ingress and egress, meaning we had the legal authority to go on the property for surveying purposes prior to closing on the land. It also gave us the legal authority to start selling lots to customers, with the sales contracts subject to our closing with the farmer and the bank. This gave us a jump start on potential payments coming in, which helped with our payments to the farmer and the bank. I don't remember how many we sold prior to closing, but it was probably around three or four sales. What a blessing to have that money coming in, since the payments to the farmer and the bank combined were over $4,000 per month—no pressure though, right?

## THE FIRST GUT PUNCH

With the property closed and the selling underway, we were off and running. Our base sales office was in Nicoma Park. Paul decided to put a second office in Jones, so he bought the building that had previously been the Rexall Drug Store. I spent a lot of time there growing up, waiting for my mom to pick me up after baseball practice. Bart moved to the Jones office and became the sales manager. I stayed at the Nicoma Park office and helped Paul manage it. We bought more land, and before long we'd really started to grow.

Sales in our Sleepy Meadows subdivision were strong. When we had two-thirds sold out with about seven permits issued, Oklahoma City intervened. They said the property was not zoned for five-acre tracts and should only have one mobile home per 40 acres. Ouch! Dad was the realtor we'd used to buy the land, so I called him. He checked his file and found where they said it was zoned for five-acre tracts.

But after checking with OKC, he saw another change to the zoning ordinance that had been previously overlooked.

We were in trouble. I went to Oklahoma City, and they told me it could be rezoned, but I would need to talk to Joe Covey and Bud Kaiser, both of whom worked in the planning and zoning department. These men were very helpful throughout the whole process. I filled out the application, then went to the courthouse to start getting names and addresses of all the surrounding property owners. After conducting my research at the courthouse, I discovered there were around 38 people who had to be notified by certified mail that we were rezoning the property. Meanwhile, Bart got all the property owners who had bought property from us to sign saying they wanted the property rezoned. The application was presented, meaning our next step was to go before the OKC City Council.

Bart and I arrived early to OKC the morning of the council meeting. Dad knew Jack Cornet, one of the council members, who told Dad to have me meet him about 15 minutes before the meeting so I could discuss what we were trying to do. I explained to Jack what had happened and why we were having to rezone the property. Thankfully, no one came to protest, but an adjoining property owner did show up to the meeting to ask what our intentions were. Once I'd explained everything to her, she was satisfied and left the meeting. That alone was a blessing—just *one* protestor could have prevented the rezoning.

Since the property was in my name, I had to be the one to stand before the council and explain what we were trying to do. When I walked up to the podium, one of the council members said, "Are you the developer?" I said, "Yes, sir!" Judging by the look on his face, you could tell he was in shock seeing that *I* was the developer. I was 20 at this time, but I looked 15!

I made my case before the mayor and the city council. Mayor Patience Latting looked over the request and told us that when a property was rezoned within OKC city limits, the city required the property owner to give up an additional 17 feet in case the city ever wanted to four-lane the existing roads. She tabled the rezoning for 30 days to give me time to have the property owners sign off their 17 feet. Bart and I felt so defeated walking out of the meeting. We met Paul and Dad back at our land office in Jones, and Dad said, "Didn't you plead your case?" I was thinking, *How am I going to overrule the mayor?!*

We got almost all the owners with property fronting on the two county roads to sign. Only three refused. One additional owner agreed to sign, but he said he wanted to tell the City Council how unhappy he was over giving up his 17 feet first. It was starting to get real interesting!

## THE FINAL SHOWDOWN ON THE REZONING

Once again, Bart and I arrived early to the next meeting. A few of the property owners were there. I looked over at the doors to the entry and saw Joe Covey waving me over to him. I walked out into the hall with him, and he told me that one of the property owners had called him and said he hadn't signed to okay the rezoning. I told Joe he had signed it and that I had the paper with his signature in my hand. Joe said, "I believe you—I just wanted you to be prepared in case this comes up." By then, the pressure was mounting.

When it was time for the council to hear our case, they asked if there was anyone who wanted to speak. One property owner, Ray—who had said he would sign, but he wanted them to know he wasn't happy about it—got up and voiced his displeasure for way too long. Jack Cornet looked at me with a face that said, "Get this guy to be quiet, he's not helping." I was sitting behind Ray, so I whispered to him, "Ray, I think they get it." Thankfully, he sat down. Whew, a small victory!

Next, I got up and said, "Mayor Latting, we got everyone to agree to give up their 17 feet. Only three people refused." After a little discussion, she made a motion to approve the rezoning, minus the three refusals. That meant those three property owners could not legally put any type of home on their lot without going through the same process we had just gone through. I looked back at Joe Covey and Bud Kaiser, and they said, "Jackie, you gave them a chance."

After that, the motion was seconded and approved! Man, it felt like Mount Everest had been lifted off my back! We were so happy and grateful. When I look back now, I realize how devastating the situation could have been: unhappy property owners, possible lawsuits, and no way to repay the bank and farmers without being able to sell the land in five-acre tracts. God is always faithful, and this was a major hurdle. I learned that no matter what blindsides us in life, we must never give up. We must trust and keep moving forward.

But we weren't done yet—there was more to come. Hang on—things were about to get wild, or as Paul would say, "Things are about to get western!"

## THE AUCTIONEERS

My father-in-law had always wanted to learn how to be an auctioneer. Likewise, Bart had considered going to an auctioneer school in Missouri. Being an auctioneer, though, was the farthest thing from my mind. One day, Paul said, "Boys, we're going to auctioneer school." I told Paul I didn't want to go to auctioneer school, and he said, "No, I'm paying for it and you're going!"

So I reluctantly went. There was a man named Sonny Phillips who had an antique store right next to Furr's cafeteria in Norman, Oklahoma. He charged $650 per person for a two-week auctioneer course, and you went every weeknight. We learned all about "number rolls" and "filler words." I've got to admit, it was very interesting. Sonny also taught us that *everything* has value if you know what to look for.

One night, he brought out a little toy tractor—you could tell it was old because it had one wheel missing. Then he asked each of us to guess the value of the toy tractor. We all guessed somewhere in the range of $10-$75.

Sonny told us it was worth $800, and if the other wheel had been kept intact, it would have been worth $4,000. Wow! He even had a book with a picture of the tractor to show us its value. We had a lot of fun and made good friends with the other students who attended that class. We all graduated, and I still have my certificate. We were dubbed "Colonels" after graduation, which is the name given to an auctioneer.

Something else interesting happened on the night we graduated. We were all planning to meet at a restaurant a couple of miles away. As I walked out of the school to my car, I heard a loud clang. I looked toward the noise and saw Paul speed off in his Lincoln Continental. I thought, *That's interesting.*

When I arrived at the restaurant shortly thereafter, there was no sign of Paul. I said to everyone, "I bet he got mixed up and went to the wrong restaurant." This was in the days of no cell phones, so I left to find him.

I found him half a mile from the auctioneer school, on the side of a major road in Norman. He'd pulled over a truck and was holding a young teenage boy at bay. The police showed up around the same time I did. Apparently, three teenage boys had stolen the newspaper machine from the sidewalk in front of the school, Paul had seen it and went off in hot pursuit. He followed them at a high rate of speed through neighborhoods, up sidewalks, and through people's yards. When they came out on the main road, they finally blew a tire. Two of them ran out through a pasture. The one Paul had detained was about 14 years old, and he was smarting off to the police. He also had a pocket full of cash. We may never know, but I believe my father-in-law's actions might have saved that young man. I had to share that story to showcase the type of man Paul is. He's a cowboy through and through!

I've been a licensed auctioneer now for 40 years. Some of my greatest joys have been the charity auctions we've done to help kids raise money. Once again, the value of my father-in-law's great mentorship is priceless!

# THE BUYOUT

Around this time, Paul had partnered with attorneys—Don Manner and Frank Pickle—on two rural land developments. The first one, called Tanglewood, was one of the developments we were selling when I first started working for Paul. We did such a great job that the attorneys wanted to develop more land with Paul. They bought another 400 acres together, called Rolling Meadows, and we started selling that development too.

Later, after most of the second development was sold, the partners decided they wanted to execute a buyout. They arranged a meeting with Paul, and I went with him. Prior to the meeting, Paul talked to the bank and got a verbal commitment from his lender to buy them out if necessary. Paul's attorney couldn't come, so it was just Paul and me.

Paul started the meeting by setting his tape recorder on the table. "Gentlemen, my attorney couldn't be here, and I have a third-grade education. So today, this tape recorder will be my attorney." Then he turned on the recorder. "Don Manners, are you present?"

"Yes," Don said.

Paul said, "Frank Pickle, are you present?"

"Yes," Frank said.

Then Paul told them he was willing to buy or sell, and that his bank had given him a commitment. The attorneys tried to negotiate buying Paul out at a low price, but he was not willing to sell for that cheap. Finally, Paul said, "Here's what I'll take: I want $35,000 from each of you, and you can buy me out of the two projects. Mr. Manners, do you agree to buy me out for $35,000?"

He said, "Yes."

Then Paul said, "Mr. Pickle, do you agree to buy me out for $35,000?"

He said, "Yes," too, and that was that!

It was amazing watching Paul negotiate. My friend Rob Roberts says, "You don't get what you deserve—you get what you negotiate." When we were done, Don Manners walked up to Paul and said, "Paul, you might only have a third-grade education, but you are a master at negotiating."

# FUNNY STORIES

*"Everything is funny, as long as it's
happening to someone else."*
Will Rogers

**DURING THE EARLY DAYS OF** my career, we were willing to try anything to boost sales. One important thing was to never miss a potential customer when they called. Remember, this was a pre-digital-technology era before cell phones! We had a landline phone, and we ran ads in all the local newspapers.

I remember when we bought our first answering machine. I told Bart we had to get creative with the voice recording, because when we first set it up, people would call and leave a message saying, "I'm not talking to no dang machine!" That made me think, *You just did talk to a machine by leaving that message!*

One day, I came up with a message that ended up being a hit! We used it all the way through our land sales days. In my Oklahoma drawl, I recorded: "Howdy! My name's Jackie Listen. Me and my 'ol brother Bart can't be at the phone at the present time, but if you're looking for some pretty land, we've got it! Or if you just want to talk to us, we want to talk to you! So, at the sound of the tone, please leave your name and number, and we'll be glad to return your call. We sure do thank you!" People would call and ask us, "Could I call back just to listen to that again?" It was hilarious—a true hit.

One day, Bart sold five acres of land to a guy named Tom. Tom worked for Southwestern Bell, where he finished work each night at midnight. Bart met Tom at the land office after he got off work one night, then sold him the land. Tom put $10,000 down, and we traded

Jackie's first business card

with him to have him install an intercom system for Paul's new horse barn. We closed with Tom, and when he came to the ranch to install the intercom system, I went up to the barn to check on him. He was sort of a comedian, and he said, "Yeah, when I heard your and Bart's recording, I thought, now there's a couple of ole country boys who either know what they're doing, or they don't."

I said, "Tom, we've got your money, and you're working here installing our intercom system—what do you think?"

"I think you Listen boys know what you're doing," he said, and we had a big laugh!

Another day, a man named Norm called and said he had a Greyhound bus that he'd converted to a motorhome. He asked if we wanted to trade it for some land. I asked him how much he wanted for the bus, and he said $15,000. We were interested, so I set an appointment for him and his wife Norma to come out the following Saturday.

That Saturday morning, I had a small sales meeting with two young salesmen we were training at the time. I told them, "I'm trading for the bus today!"

Then Norm showed up without Norma. I said, "Norm, where's Norma?" and he said, "She gave me the authority to negotiate today!"

I said, "Great!" After that, I toured him around. He decided to buy four two-and-a-half-acre tracts. When the dust settled, I'd given him $15,000 for the bus and financed $40,000. We needed Norma's signature on the contract, so I followed Norm to his house. When we walked into the house, he had me stay in his dining room so he could explain to Norma the terms of the contract. He said, "Norma, we just bought ten acres of land for $55,000!" She said, "$55,000 for ten acres?!" He said, "Yes, but he's giving us $15,000 as a trade for the bus!"

Immediately, Norma said, "Where do I sign!"

I then drove Norm to a local RV dealership where he had the bus on consignment. Norm said, "I'll let you drive." I said, "Let me just follow you for now. I'll learn to drive the bus later!" So, I followed him back to the office, and I still remember the look of pure disbelief on the faces of my two salesmen as the bus rolled into the lot!

# TRADING

"A joyful heart is good medicine, but a
crushed spirit dries up the bones."
Proverbs 17:22

**MY FATHER-IN-LAW HAS ALWAYS SAID,** "I'd just as soon trade as eat!"
As a young man, Paul was taught how to trade by an older gentleman.
Paul has been self-employed most of his life and has always made a
living buying and selling. He taught Bart and I how to trade as well.
One time, Paul traded for a small airplane. The man who owned it
said, "Paul, I'll take you for a flight in my plane." Paul said, "I'm going
to take your word on everything about the plane. No need for a test
flight!"

I could tell you countless funny stories about Paul's trading abilities,
but I'll stick to a few:

Paul had what he called a "bone yard," which was a fenced yard behind
our office where we would put all our trade items. Since we owner-
financed most of our sales, people would often have something to
trade for their down payment. We traded for horses, sheep, a plane,
an in-ground swimming pool, lake lots, cars, motorcycles, etc. One
day, Paul said, "Run an ad. The bone yard is full!"

We had an old 1957 boat with big fins on it like those cars from the
'50s. The man who traded it to us told us the motor had run fine
the last time he'd had it in the water. We ran an ad selling the boat
for $500, and soon we started getting calls. One Saturday, I spoke
to a man who asked about the boat. I said, "Sir, we traded for the
boat as is, and we're selling it that way." I told him everything the
man who'd given us the boat had said. I then told him, "Sir, I'll also
tell you … this boat is ugly!" Still, he told me he wanted to come in
and look at it.

So, I set a time to meet. He came in, and I said, "It's out back here in our yard."

I barely got to the gate before he said, "Is that the boat?"

I replied, "Yes."

He said, "It's ugly!"

I said, "I told you it was ugly!"

I opened the gate for him. As he circled the boat, he kept saying, "It's so ugly!" He then pulled on the motor a couple of times and said, "What about the motor?" I went back over everything I'd told him on the phone, how we had traded for the boat, and how the man said the last time he had it in the water that it ran. Finally, I laughed and told him, "The last time it ran could've been 1957. He didn't tell me the year."

We both laughed. Finally, he said, "You guys are asking $500 for this ugly boat?"

"Yes, sir. But if you want to make an offer, we'll let you."

He said, "I'm afraid to make an offer. I'm afraid I'll own this ugly thing!"

After that, I asked him to come into the office, meet Paul, and have a cup of coffee. He and Paul visited for a minute, then Paul said, "What about the boat?"

The man said, "It's ugly! I can't believe you're asking $500!"

Paul said, "I'm over 21, so just make me an offer. You won't hurt my feelings!"

The man said, "I'm afraid I'll own it!" I was sitting there thinking, *If he does make an offer, it's going to be for $25!* But finally, the man said, "I'll give you $250."

Paul said, "How are you going to pay me—with an 'ol bad check, or with cash?"

He said, "Cash" and Paul said, "Sold!"

"Ohhhhhh no!" the man groaned.

He paid Paul in cash, and the boat was his! So, he took his brand-new Olds Cutlass and hooked the ugly boat to it. Just before he left the parking lot, he said to me, "I'm going to my shop, taking off the motor, and I hope it works. Then I'm taking the boat to the lake and sinking it!" We both laughed, and then off he went!

Another time, a man drove his motorcycle out to the office on a cold January day. I took him on a land tour and found an acreage he wanted to buy. Paul traded for his motorcycle, then told the man, "I'm going to see how tough my son-in-law is by letting him ride home on the back of your motorcycle. Then he can drive it back." I said, "Paul, why don't I just take him home in my nice warm Jeep?" We all laughed, and then I drove him home in the Jeep!

There are tons and tons more stories I could tell. Looking back, it was a lot of fun. People always enjoyed trading and negotiating.

## FLEETWOOD SALESMAN

During the 1980s, banks would not loan to individuals on small acreages. Because we would owner-finance, we had a corner on the market for raw land. Our underwriting at that time was also much easier for an individual to qualify (compared to going to a bank). We were constantly looking for ways to create more cash (so we could pay down more of the debt on our developments). Paul knew a man named Jim who went to church with us, and Jim had approached Paul about becoming a Fleetwood mobile home dealer. Doing so would allow us to buy homes at a discount and include the acreage in the financing, which is typically called a "land package deal."

The advantages for us were two-fold. We would make profit on the mobile home and cash out the acreage. Paul and Jim decided to partner and became a Fleetwood dealer. We were experiencing tremendous growth and expansion, but we'd all bitten off more than we could chew. So, our plan was to have Jim manage the Fleetwood division of our company, which meant ordering homes, setting up the homes, and arranging the financing. Jim's son and son-in-law were also going to be working with him. Paul, Bart, and I would be handling the sales and marketing side, although Paul was also managing a sales office in Kellyville, Oklahoma (a two-hour drive from our home). He had purchased 240 acres in that area and was selling a development he'd named Graceland Ranchettes. So, it was just Bart and I selling in the Jones area.

We started by ordering two double-wides as speculation homes, which meant taking a risk and hoping we could find buyers for them. These double-wides would also serve as model homes that we could show potential customers. We set each one up on a one-acre tract that Paul owned, then we ordered two more double-wides.

One day, before either of the homes had been sold, Jim walked into my office with a box and said, "I'm moving my family to Texas. Here's all the information you'll need on the double-wides."

"I don't know anything about this," I told him.

"It's easy. All the information is there in that box," he said. I found out later that "easy" was an understatement! I called Paul and told him what had happened. Obviously, Paul was not thrilled about it.

So there we were: three workers short, with two new homes on the way and no one to set them up. Paul called and got the two new orders stopped, which Fleetwood was not happy about. I immediately started finding out what type of financing was available and discovered the financing was not as easy as it was presented. The one avenue available was a government-backed loan, which required a ton of paperwork. The borrower's credit score also had to be tremendously high to qualify, which eliminated many of our potential buyers. Bottom line, we were totally blindsided by Jim bailing and moving to Texas. We suddenly had two double-wides to sell, and this whole new division was now my responsibility. I had to learn everything from scratch. It was a rough road to travel.

One thing I've come to learn: I was being stretched. And as my mentor Dr. Bob Terry taught me, once your box is stretched, it never goes back. This was going to be a box-stretching moment.

Late in 1983, when the economy was still good, I was fortunate to meet a woman named Audrey. She and her husband were moving from Missouri. Her husband had been diagnosed with cancer, and they needed to be close to her daughter. Audrey and her husband had owned a Ben Franklin five-and-dime store and had sold it for good money. She had cash to pay for some land and a double-wide.

I showed Audrey one of our new Fleetwoods, and she decided to order one. We struck a package deal for five acres and ordered the new home. Audrey loved the land. It reminded her of where she'd grown up in Missouri. The front four acres were flat, and the back acre sloped down into a beautiful valley with trees. The back acre was where she wanted the double-wide to go. Getting the double-wide there was challenging, so we hired a man with a dozer, and he was able to get it positioned on the concrete runners. Jim's son and son-in-law hadn't moved to Texas yet, so we hired them to set it up. Their crew went to work, and I went by one day to check on the progress. When I walked into the house, I felt like I was leaning.

"It's not level," I told them.

"Oh no, it's level."

"Get the level out and let's see."

One of them put the level on the floor, and it was so far off that it wasn't even funny. I told them they'd have to redo it, and they decided they couldn't finish the house—so they quit.

Now what? I called the dealership and was put in touch with their warranty technician. He told us what he would charge, and we hired him to come up from Texas to finish our project. He had to totally start over, but when he was done, it was done right! I learned a tremendous amount through this short-lived Fleetwood dealership adventure. Audrey taught me that if you always hold back paying the final amount until the job is complete, you have a better chance of a contractor finishing the job. Our character was good, so we would have completed any job regardless—but I've still always remembered what she taught me

We sold one more double-wide and got it financed through the tedious process of a government-backed loan. In total, we sold four double-wide homes. One was a cash sale, two were financed, and the last one Paul had to owner-finance. The economy had started to slow, so it wasn't easy to get cashed out. The last one we got financed, the terms were for 30 years at 16.25% interest—ouch!

Paul and I learned a valuable lesson on these: They were *not* our niche!

## THE RENT HOUSES

One day, I walked into our land office and Bart said, "I found us a deal."

An older couple had come in and told Bart they wanted out of Oklahoma. They had five rental houses on 3.5 acres of land in Jones. They said they would take $50,000 for all of it. Paul came to the office, and the three of us went out to look at them. There were four small 1,000-square-foot, two-bedroom, one-bath houses built in the 1940s, plus one 1,400-square-foot house that sat behind the four. The couple lived in the larger house and rented the front four out for $300 a piece per month. I wasn't sure about the deal, but we agreed together to buy them. Boy, we were getting ready to get an education on these!

The day we closed, all the renters moved out except for one nice, older couple. So we went to work renting. Since we were green in the rental business and very trusting, we thought everyone would tell us the truth. Bart oversaw the project, and he rented them all out quickly. I was helping Paul some in Tulsa at this time, plus trying to help put out other fires with our business. When the first rent payments were due, the excuses started: "My grandmother passed away," "We just don't have the money," "I lost my job," or "We're just a little short this month, but we can catch up next month." The list goes on.

There were more excuses the following month. Some renters just up and moved out, and they took things with them such as cabinet doors, toilets, and light fixtures. You name it—they took it. Plus, we didn't have any lease agreements in writing—ouch! I know that's hard to believe, but you have to remember that this was our first rental property experience, and our education was just beginning. It reminds me of a story a good friend of mine, Ivan Goodman, once told me. He was a very successful real estate investor in Norman. During the start of his investment career, he and his brother wanted to open a machine shop. His wife, Betty, was against it. She advised him not to open it. Ivan said, "We did it anyway."

About one year later, it wasn't making any money. So they had to shut it down. He knew that evening that he was going to have to tell Betty. He said, "I walked in and said, 'Betty, we shut down the machine shop today.' She didn't say a word. She walked over and got out a yellow tablet and drew a line down the middle. Then she started writing and said, 'We'll put this experience on the education side of the column!'" This project was definitely going to be an education.

We found out later that three of the houses had 75-gallon septic tanks that had to be pumped every two months. Three of the houses also shared one water well. The heat and air units were old and had not been cleaned in a long time. We suddenly had costs we hadn't anticipated. Keep in mind we were not handymen, so everything had to be hired out. By the time we made the bank payments and paid the insurance and repair bills, it was clear we were losing money.

The lender we'd used on the homes went broke, and our loan was sold to a bank in Mustang, Oklahoma. By the time that bank called, we owed some back payments. The bank president set us up on a plan, and I worked with him every month to pay them off.

By this time, Bart had gotten his fill of managing the properties, so he said, "You try them awhile." Shortly after that, I got a call from a man moving back from California. He agreed to rent one of the houses sight unseen and sent two months' rent in advance. When he got into town, I opened the house for him only to see there'd been a water leak. I found out the hot water pipe had broken, and the previous renter had told Bart he was a plumber who would fix it in exchange for rent. But instead of a hot-water pipe, he'd installed a cold-water pipe. He'd also used a portion of a garden hose for part of the line, which had busted and flooded the house.

Honestly, the stories about these rental houses could fill another book. Here's a few more highlights:

One day, one of the renters came into the Jones land office and said, "It's a swamp out there. Come take a look." I went and met him at the property, and he was right—the ground felt like walking on a sponge. This property was high ground, not in a flood plain. I called the plumber, and he came down to the office. He told me there was a pipe coming from the well—they had used the cheap black pipe, and roots had grown into it everywhere. He said, "You have a giant soaker hose out there!" Man, it was brutal! We paid him to put in the correct type of pipe, which was expensive, especially considering all the money we were already losing. Plus, the electric bill for the water pump the next month had tripled!

Another time, I was showing a vacant house to a possible renter. The renter from the house next door came up and said he needed to talk to me. I told him I'd come talk to him in a minute. After he walked off, the young man looking to rent the house had a funny look on his face. He said, "He's got my belt buckle on." I said, "What?" He said, "Yes, someone broke into my apartment and stole some of my stuff a while back—that's my belt buckle!" I said, "Then you can go ask him for it back, but I'm not going to!" The fun never ended!

There was also the time Bart leased to a family on a Friday. They wrote the first month's rent check. On Monday, his wife called and said her husband had decided to BBQ in one of the little charcoal grills. He'd thrown some gas on the grill, and it exploded and severely burned him! We felt so bad for her—he ended up in the burn center for quite a while with third degree burns on his legs. Meanwhile, the rent check they'd written bounced. We let her stay there for several months until her husband recovered. Then they moved out, all without ever paying us a dime! About a year later, I got a call from the FBI looking for the husband!

We finally wised up and started screening possible renters. We also had some fortunate luck for once. We sold land to a man who worked for the Resolution Trust Corporation (RTC). The RTC was set up after the 1980s savings and loans crisis. The RTC became a massive property-management company, cleaning up what was, at the time, the largest collapse of U.S. financial institutions since the Great Depression.

The property owner we'd sold to worked as a general handyman for the RTC. When they repossessed a home, they would send him in to fix things and install all new fixtures before they put it on the market. If an existing item from the home was in good condition, they allowed him to take it, so he'd ended up with a surplus of toilets, windows, doorknobs, etc. Even though he had a good job, times were hard, and he got behind on his land payments to us. We ended up trading with him to do repair work on the renthouses in exchange for back payments on his land. He was good at what he did, and this trade ended up saving us on repair expenses while allowing him to keep his land.

Finally, we were more than ready to sell these rental properties. Our cousin Mike was a true rental property expert, so I called him one day and said, "Mike, we'd like to sell these. Come look so we can make a deal!" We negotiated a sweet deal for him, and I got him in with the banker in Mustang. Mike bought the properties, and he still owns them to this day.

One last funny story: We had rented to a man who was an equine dentist for racehorses at Remington Park racetrack in Oklahoma City. Mike called me about a month after he'd bought the properties. He had an answering machine where his renters could leave a message. He and his wife had just sat down for supper when the phone rang, so they let the answering machine pick up. They heard the equine dentist leave the following message in his cowboy, country drawl: "Mike, this is Jim ... the toilet fell through!" Mike's wife looked at him and said, "Do you think he was on it when it fell?" And Mike said, "Yes, he was on it!"

Conclusion: find your niche. This wasn't ours, but I'm grateful for the experience and happy that Mike still owns them, and we don't!

## FALLING DOMINOES

Recently, I looked up the definition of falling dominoes. The Free Dictionary describes it as such: "If things fall like dominoes, they are damaged, destroyed or defeated quickly."

The collapse of Penn Square Bank in Oklahoma City on July 5, 1982, set off a chain reaction that would result in the downfall of several large banks throughout the country. Since we didn't have any loans with them, it took a while for our business to feel the impact. But by the end of the 1980s, 139 banks in Oklahoma would fall due to Penn Square Bank becoming insolvent. Due to reduced demand, the oil boom that started in the late 1970s (and continued to the 1980s) had led to a huge oil surplus, causing the price of oil to fall by half. This resulted in the oil bust. All these events had set the dominoes in place, and once they fell, it put Oklahoma in one of the greatest recessions since the Great Depression. Everything that was coming our way was going to be outside of our control.

Paul kept expanding and buying property. From the end of 1981 to 1986, he had purchased about 3,150 acres of land, plus commercial land, rental properties, and the construction of a 14,000-square-foot shopping strip center. We were busy, working with 8 to 10 banks who understood our business and would loan us money. One funny memory I have from then is the time we purchased 80 acres. Paul had made a phone call to the president of the bank, who'd verbally okayed us a few weeks prior. When it came time to close, we had forgotten to call and get the $50,000 we needed for closing the next week. I remember at the bank, Paul was walking next to the bank president and said, "Monty, I need $50,000 to close on the 80 acres next week." Monty was on his way to the restroom, and replied, "Paul, can I go in here first?" We started laughing. The next week, we signed the papers and closed! Things were full speed ahead!

As I said, Penn Square Bank's demise in 1982 was not fully felt by our business until the fall of 1986. But looking back, I can spot little signs along the way. My first vivid recollection was a conversation I had with one of our appraisers sometime in 1985. He was delivering an appraisal, and he told me, "The Savings and Loans are going to go under in about six months. If you're going to borrow any more money, you better do it now. They're going to collapse." That was the first time I realized there was a possibility that things could get rough. And boy, was he ever right. We were about to be blindsided.

## THE SHOPPING CENTER

Limited Partnerships were the going vehicle of choice in the early 1980s. A Limited Partnership would limit your liability to a specific project—unless you were the General Partner, in which case all your personal assets were on the line. Something we didn't know—but which we learned later—is that in a Limited Partnership, at least one partner is required to be a General Partner, making them have unlimited liability.

Paul leased an office in Norman called a "mini-suite" from a man he later got to know well. This man was putting together limited partnerships and building strip shopping centers. In a portion of these shopping centers, he created mini-suites for small business owners who only needed a small office. He also provided a receptionist to answer phone calls for the lessees. He later invited Paul to partner with him on a new shopping center if Paul could find the right location. In Jones, there was a corner with good traffic. Paul talked to me and asked if I wanted to partner with them on this project. I said, "Paul I don't know about this one. I'm concerned that we are getting out of our expertise." Keep in mind, at this point we thought we would just be limited to this project.

We decided to buy the land. There were originally five partners, including Paul and myself. We borrowed the money to purchase 13 acres of land on a great corner in Jones. The plan was then to borrow money on four of those acres to build a 14,000-square-foot strip shopping center, which would result in us having nine acres of commercial land paid for. By the time all the plans and specs were put together and our partnership was set up, four partners remained. The fifth had dropped out.

We obtained our financing for the construction of the new shopping center from an institution called SISCORP. There, banks participated together on projects. The day we closed, SISCORP was booming with people. When it was our time to go in, we signed a mountain of loan papers. I remember asking one of our partners who was an Executive VP of a bank, "Is there any concern here with what we're signing?" He just mumbled something and kept signing. Oh, if we had only known and had asked for the paperwork in advance! Or if we'd taken the time to read the novel before us! But I guess hindsight is 20/20, right?

Our understanding of the loan terms was that we were financing $675,000 on a one-year construction loan at 13% interest. After the first year, once the construction was completed, we would then enter into a mini perm—meaning the loan would be put on monthly principal and interest payments—based on a 25-year payback with a five-year balloon payment.

Construction started in 1984. The final project, subject to completion, appraised at $915,000. We owed $675,000 and had nine acres paid for. We were also getting interest with possible businesses wanting to lease space in the shopping center. We had hired a general manager to oversee all the construction and to keep our contractor bids competitive.

The lender required that we call for draws to receive money on the construction loan to pay the contractors. Halfway into the project, when we submitted a draw, we discovered that SISCORP was broke! How in the world had this happened? We had $30,000 due to contractors, and now we couldn't get a draw to pay them. We all went to work trying to find out what had happened. After a few days of relentlessly trying to find any information, we learned that two banks had participated in our loan: a Savings and Loan in Woodward, Oklahoma, and a bank in Edmond, Oklahoma.

## THE SOLUTION

After finding out that two banks were involved, a meeting was set up at SISCORP. I was sent to this meeting while Paul and another partner made a surprise visit to the president of the Savings and Loan in Woodward. SISCORP had been bustling just a few months prior, but now it looked like a ghost town. There was only one employee left. He directed me back to the conference room, where I met the president of the Edmond bank, two attorneys from a high-powered law firm in Oklahoma City who were representing the bank, and a gentleman by the name of Murray, who was representing the United States government. He was referred to as the "death attorney." His job was to clean up when a financial institution went under. One thing that stuck out in my mind was that he had gold rings on both hands. He was a stocky, burly guy.

Murray led the meeting. The first question he asked is "Who are you?" I said, "One of the partners." Keep in mind, I was 24 years old at that time. He was in shock. "Well, where are the other partners?" he said. I told him they had gone to Woodward. "Well, what are they doing there?" he said. He was a grouchy guy.

"Sir, we're just trying to find out what has happened here so we can pay our contractors," I said. After that I didn't say another word—I just took notes.

We learned that the president of the Woodward Savings and Loan was on the board of SISCORP, and that they had funded $275,000 of our loan. Within SISCORP, there'd been a fair amount of embezzlement going on, which ended up bankrupting them. We found out later that as soon as the $275,000 had been funded to our loan, it disappeared—along with the money from lots of other loans. There were construction projects all over the country that had been shut down, including a $7,000,000 motel in California. The loan was not structured how we originally thought. We'd essentially signed a one-year, single-pay construction note at 13% interest, which would have been due in full at the end of that one-year term! We also found out from our legal counsel that somehow—without our knowledge—Paul had been set up as the General Partner from the very beginning. We now had a breach of contract, meaning we could have legally sued SISCORP and had the loan debt forgiven. However, we still owed $30,000 to our contractors, the shopping center was only halfway completed, and we would have had to obtain additional financing to finish construction. Plus, who knows how long a lawsuit would have tied the property up for.

The economy was still strong at this point, so after weighing all our options, we decided to negotiate with the bank in Edmond and the Savings and Loan in Woodward. We agreed to a refinance of the existing construction loan, with a good interest rate and some type of permanent financing at the end of construction. This was our best option. We could complete the project, get tenants in, and start paying down our debt. The last thing we needed was an incomplete construction project in my hometown. That would not have helped the reputation of our business.

## THE CLOSING

When the refinance was complete, we came to the bank's attorney's office to sign. One condition of the refinance was that the bank required all of us to personally endorse the note and made all of us General Partners (even our wives). Remember, in a Limited Partnership, your personal assets are not on the line unless you are a General Partner, which we were not aware of at the time. This put all our personal assets up for collateral, which had been my initial concern in the beginning. And now our wives were also personally responsible.

On the day of closing, they dropped one more bombshell on us: we had a $23,200 interest payment due—ouch! Sure, I was young and inexperienced—but if I'd known what we were signing that day, I would have never signed.

Lesson learned: never enter into an agreement without first having legal counsel review what you're signing. This way, you'll understand the risk involved. Trust me, you do not want to learn the hard way like we did!

# RED SEA MIRACLES

**March 21, 1986**

*"And Moses said unto the people, Fear ye not, stand
still, and see the salvation of God." Exodus 14:13*

**WITH OUR LOAN NOW INCREASED** to $698,200 (because of the $23,200 of accrued interest), the project was back on track for completion. Originally, we had planned and gotten approval for a septic system for the shopping center due to a sewer system moratorium that we thought the state of Oklahoma had on the city of Jones. For a building that large, the lateral lines would have taken up two whole acres of our prime commercial land. And in a commercial project like this, city sewer far outweighs a septic system.

But before we had installed the septic system, we discovered at a city council meeting that there was a possibility we could tie into the city's sewer system. One of the council members explained that they had a problem that needed to be fixed before we could connect to their sewer lines. Paul asked how big of a problem, and they said they thought there was around 90 feet of sewer line that needed to be fixed. At the meeting that evening, we agreed to fix the sewer line issue, and in turn they would allow us to tie in. But after consulting with an engineer and our contractor, we found out it was actually *600 feet* of line that needed to be fixed—not 90. Along with our 2,000 feet of sewer line needed to connect to the city's sewer system, the whole project would cost just shy of $60,000. While our budget had factored in the cost of installing a septic system, this amount far exceeded what we had originally planned. We suddenly were tasked with coming up with additional money that we didn't have. No pressure!

A few months later, on a Saturday morning, Paul was visiting with Bart and I at our land office in Jones. Usually, Paul was at his office in

Norman or selling land at his office in Kellyville. And while he was in Jones that morning, a man named Grady Delling walked in the door. Grady owned several small rural grocery stores called Country Boy IGA. Grady wanted to buy the two acres we had originally planned to put the septic system on and instead put a grocery store on the land! I watched while Paul sold the two acres to Grady for $60,000 in about 30 minutes! Monday morning, we were at Grady's office with a contract. I told Grady he was my first employer in high school. I'd worked for him long enough to save money and buy my first set of auto body tools.

About 30 days later, we were at the closing company ready to close when Grady pulled Paul and I over to the side. He explained how he could tell if a community was ready for a grocery store by having the electric company run a count on how many meters there were in a certain area. If the meter count met Grady's criteria, then the community was ready. Originally the meter count showed that Jones could support a store, but he said that he had it rerun and had just gotten the report back. For some reason, the numbers weren't as high as they'd originally reported, meaning the area wasn't quite ready. He wanted to back out on the land. My heart sank, but Paul stayed calm and said, "Grady, when I met you, I knew you were a man of your word."

Grady looked at Paul, and there was a long silence. Then he said, "You're right Paul. I'm buying the land!"

Whew! That's what I like to call a "Red Sea miracle."

See, in the Bible, when the children of Israel were fleeing Egypt, they found themselves standing at the Red Sea. There was nowhere to go, and Pharoah's army was in pursuit behind them. God told Moses in Exodus 14 to "stand still and see the salvation of God." When Moses extended his staff over the water, the Red Sea parted, and they were able to walk across on dry land. In my life, I've seen many instances where there looks to be nowhere to go and no options in sight, but then a miracle happens. That's why I refer to these moments as Red Sea miracles. And this was just one of many to come.

To recap, Grady had popped in on a day where Paul *just happened* to be at our office. The electric company showed that the community was ready, but then the count was wrong—coincidence? I don't think so! We now had the money to pay our contractor, the sewer issue was solved, and we didn't have to borrow more money.

## THE BOTTOM IS GETTING READY TO FALL

We have a local amusement park here in Oklahoma City called Frontier City. At the park, there's a ride that has a large barrel. You step into the barrel, stand against the wall, and then get spun around and around like an old dryer until the bottom of the barrel drops out, leaving everyone thrown against the walls. It's an eerie feeling to be suspended like that with nothing below you! Little did we know that the bottom was getting ready to drop out of sight for us.

When the shopping center was near completion, Paul thought it would be wise to buy the land immediately across the street (to the east) from it. We were improving the area and knew that land prices would start to increase. Paul had borrowed his limit at the bank, so my wife and I took out a personal loan in the fall of 1985. We purchased 20 acres of commercial land with Paul and Alma as our partners. This land also had an old two-story house on it that the local doctor had lived in. This was a very prestigious house in its day, one I'd admired since I was a little boy.

We borrowed $160,000 at 14% interest, set up on a single pay note. A single pay note means that the principal balance of the loan and the interest are due in full at the end of the loan term, which in this case was one year. The bank will often take a payment and renegotiate the loan another year, but they are not legally obligated to extend the loan.

By the fall of 1986, our business really started going south. General Motors had begun making massive layoffs. Savings and Loans were going under, just as our appraiser had predicted. The oil bust caused banks to close, and people were filing for bankruptcy and moving out of the state to find jobs. Every day, I opened the newspaper and saw pages of foreclosures and bankruptcies. You were hard-pressed to find anything positive or uplifting during that time. Paul's business went from around 600 property owners (who paid him monthly payments for the mortgages we held) to around 300 property owners. Our clients either filed for bankruptcy or just moved away, abandoning the land along with the debt they owed us. During this time, the economy in the rest of the United States was recovering, and people were leaving Oklahoma and going back to the states they'd originally come from. Our cash flow decreased dramatically, to the point where you could hardly give land away for free in Oklahoma.

Around eight months into the loan, we had no sales prospects. The weight was really bearing down on me. We had put a "For Sale" sign out on the corner of the property advertising 1 to 20 acres for sale. We were willing to break the land up and sell any amount.

I was sitting at our land office one day when I received a call from a lady named Mrs. B. She asked me to tell her about our land on the corner. She said, "You're a Christian, aren't you?" I responded, "Ma'am I'm trying to be." She told me that she was a pastor with a church in Midwest City, Oklahoma, and that God had shown her in a dream some land east of Jones. She said, "This is not the land he showed me, but I felt the presence of God when I drove by your sign."

I proceeded to tell her about the land, and I set up a time to meet that afternoon with her and her husband. As I mentioned before, the land had an old farmhouse on it that—at the time it was built—had been one of the more prestigious homes in our community. With commercial property, if an existing structure can't be converted for business purposes, it's typically more profitable to tear the structure down. Though we did consider that, we hadn't done anything with the house yet. And I'm so glad we hadn't, because I could tell Mrs. B and her husband were very interested in it. I could also tell that Mr. B was the businessman of the two.

He and I sat down and chewed the fat. Throughout the course of our conversation, I learned that they were originally from Covington,

Indiana. That area had recently experienced a recession, and they had not been able to sell. Mr. B was a brilliant fabricator and had done quite a bit of work on their home in Indiana. He said they were interested in buying the farmhouse and about nine acres, and he told me they liked to trade. My father-in-law always said he'd just as soon trade as eat, so I set up a meeting with Paul.

That evening, Paul and I went to their home and had a wonderful visit. When we left, we had a signed contract. We traded for their home in Covington, Indiana, along with a $30,000 down payment for the house and nine acres of commercial land, with an additional $7,500 due the following year.

I can't tell you the weight this took off my shoulders. It felt like an anvil being lifted. I was able to walk into the bank and pay $30,000 towards interest and principal on that single pay loan. As I handed the check over to the bank president, he asked me when the payment was due, and I told him, "Four days ago." The bank renewed the loan, and we were able to survive another year.

We now owned a house in Indiana, which we knew might be challenging to sell given the state's economy. We found a local realtor in the area who was willing to list it for us. The realtor thought the house would sell for anywhere from $70,000-$80,000. It was a 4000-square-foot home with a basement that had been moved out of a highway easement. Mr. B had made quite a few improvements to the home. After some time, the realtor finally got a contract on the home for $70,000. We flew into Indianapolis when it was time to close. The realtor picked us up and asked if we were ready to see the house. Paul said "I don't want to see the house. I just want to see a check in my hand." We went straight to closing, got our cashier's check, and boarded a plane back to Oklahoma that evening without ever laying eyes on the house! The next day, I walked that check into the bank to pay another payment on the loan. The president couldn't believe it. "Can I fly you guys anywhere else?" he asked. I told him we'd fly anywhere we needed to get that loan paid off.

Eventually, we did pay it off.

## SEPTEMBER, 1986

The shopping center was finally completed in the fall of 1986. Since the economy was still falling, all our interested pre-leases backed out. I'd been tasked with leasing, completing, and overseeing any construction needed for the new potential tenants. By that point, we had a pizza restaurant, a donut shop, an arcade room, a church, an insurance agency, and a family video store.

Our partner—who was a bank executive—was fired from his position in September of 1986. He later filed for bankruptcy. Our investor partner also filed for bankruptcy in November of 1986. This left Paul and I holding the bag! We took our last draw of $43,000 to pay the last bid of contractors on October 1, 1986. A few days later, the Woodward Savings and Loan that had participated in our loan went under.

Everyone was trying to survive those tough times. Someone once told me, "People do funny things when they are drowning." When you experience a down economy that affects everyone, and everything is deteriorating right before your eyes, it's hard to find hope. These men did what they had to do, and so did many others in our state.

# THE CARD

*"A word of encouragement during a failure is worth*
*more than an hour of praise after success."*
Unknown

**THE MORNING OF OCTOBER 3,** 1986, Paula sent me to work with a card. When I got to the office, I sat down at my desk and opened the envelope. On the front was this little soldier holding both arms up, carrying shields in each hand, with arrows flying at him from both sides. I thought, *That's me!* Then I opened the card and read it. It said, "Life could be boring! Love, Paula." I started dying laughing. She also wrote, "You do the very best you can do, and God will bless you according to your faithfulness and effort." And she gave these two scriptures: Mark 8:1-9 and Mark 8:34.

I still have that little card today. It was so special and encouraging—a bright light during a moment of darkness. It was rough trying to keep my mindset right and not dwell on everything coming against us. It's hard to explain in words how failure tries to beat you up when you are going through difficult times. Little golden nuggets of hope like that card, and God, are what got me through. I've learned now as a "Chief Encouragement Officer" how important hope really is. My wife's obedience to buy that card and provide the right words of encouragement and scripture was a major turning point at that time. And because I kept that card, I can share this wisdom with you today.

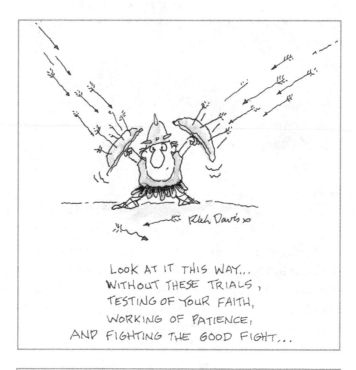

The card that Paula gave to Jackie

## MAXINE KINCHELOE PROPERTY TAX LAW

The economy was still getting worse. As the saying goes, "One thing leads to another." While we allowed mobile homes on the acreages that people were buying from us, we didn't finance them. That meant we had no information on them. We didn't know the make, model, who it was financed through, etc. During this time, the tag agency required a tag to be purchased for a mobile home, much like a car. You paid tax in the beginning and purchased a tag each year. Maxine Kincheloe was in the Oklahoma House of Representatives during this time. She saw that schools were losing tax revenue on mobile homes, since the tax money was going to tag agencies instead of the county. Representative Kincheloe pushed for a bill (that passed) requiring all mobile homes to be put over on the ad valorem tax rolls through the county assessors' offices. It was a great idea, but the timing was awful for us. People were abandoning the land, along with their mobile homes. The county assessors' offices knew there was a mobile home on the land, but they had no information on it. At the exact same time, the mobile homes were being repossessed by the lenders and moved off the property. This law created a huge workload for each county. With no information on the mobile homes, they would go out to assess and would often find that the mobile home was no longer there. They would then simply estimate what they thought five acres with a mobile home was worth on average, then start billing us as the mortgage holder.

If property taxes were delinquent at that time, anyone could pay the taxes and buy what was called a "tax certificate." If they did that for three to four consecutive years, they could then apply for a tax deed. Properties with delinquent taxes owed on them did not go to tax sale back then, as they would today.

Here's where it got really tough on us. Since we sold and deeded the land, then carried back an owner-financed mortgage, we acted as the bank. The dilemma was that they were putting the mobile home tax burden over on us as the mortgage holder, but we had no financial interest in the mobile home. This obviously wasn't fair. They also started charging high interest rates and late penalties on the mobile homes. We had delinquent tax bills coming in for these mobile homes that we had no ownership interest in, and we couldn't pay them. We also ran the risk of an individual paying the delinquent taxes for tax certificates, which could have caused us to lose our land—all over a mobile home that was never ours to begin with!

I started calling the assessors' offices in the different counties where we had developments to tell them that the mobile homes were no longer on many of the lots. That stopped any future tax assessment as far as each mobile home was concerned, but not the back tax. I remember telling them, "Billing us isn't fair. We never had anything to do with the mobile homes."

They replied, "I know, but we don't know who else to bill except for the landowner or the mortgage holder."

This whole dilemma would never have fallen on us if the lenders who'd financed the mobile homes had paid their 936 forms. (A 936 form required the lender to furnish the county with all the information on the mobile home, and it would have told them where the home was being moved to.) Most of the lenders who had financed these mobile homes were Savings and Loans, which were going out of business daily.

If the bumps in the road our business had already endured weren't enough, this whole ordeal started hitting us from a different direction. It felt like being in a war where you're surrounded, but you still don't have a clue where the next shell is coming from. One thing was leading to another, and at every turn it seemed the unfairness and responsibility was falling on our shoulders. Hang on, it gets even more interesting!

We were suddenly forced into being private investigators—tracking down and finding out anything we could to trace the mobile homes back to the lenders. If we could find the lender and they were solvent, we could get the money to pay the mobile home back tax. Keep in mind the hardship we were facing. At this point we had no income on an acreage that we couldn't sell, because it was not in our name.

We couldn't afford to lose it to a tax deed, so we had no choice but to grind it out and get the back taxes paid.

Here's an example of what we were dealing with. One day, I was sitting in our office. I'd been working on a mobile home tax for several months, and I'd finally tracked it down to a Savings and Loan. They agreed they owed the bill, but by the time they said they would pay, they had closed. This happened *twice* with that same mobile home. And as I was sitting there that day, I got a call from a gentleman at Kingfisher Savings and Loan. He told me who he was and asked if it was okay if he got another person on the phone with me, since they had some questions. I said sure.

This man gave me his name and said he was in Washington, D.C. He said, "Mr. Listen, it's my understanding you've been having some issues trying to get some back taxes paid, is this correct?"

"Yes, sir," I said.

He said, "Mr. Listen, how much is the amount?" The way he was asking, it was like he was expecting a six-figure amount.

"Around $1,700.00."

"Oh, that is not a problem," he said. Then he told the other gentlemen at the Savings and Loan to fill out a certain form number and send it to me. After that, he said, "Mr. Listen, is there anything else?"

I said no. He thanked me, then turned me back to the man who had called me, who put me on hold. He came back on the next moment and verified my address. Then he asked, "Mr. Listen, can I tell you something?" I said sure, and he said, "I would like to commend you on your persistence in this matter. Most people would have given up."

"Sir, that wasn't an option. I didn't have the money to pay for this!"

He laughed and thanked me, and I thanked him as well. A few days later, I received the check to pay the taxes. Whew, what a relief!

## TAX REFORM ACT OF 1986

Just when we thought our obstacles couldn't get any more challenging, the Federal Government passed The Tax Reform Law of 1986. There were good things in this bill, but it's effect on us was devastating. Our accountant explained to us that it had to do with passive and non-passive income. Here's what an article from the Los Angeles Times explained:

> "When Congress enacted the Tax Reform Act of 1986, it established a new concept called 'passive activities.' Although the primary motivation for the new law as it affected real estate was to curtail the tax-shelter abuse, the net result was a dramatic impact on the average real estate investor."

We were the "average investor." Prior to 1986, we enjoyed what we called "installment sales." An installment sale under the rules of Generally Accepted Accounting Principles (GAAP) accounts for when revenue and expense are recognized at the time of cash collection (in our case, that meant the monthly payment) rather than at the time of sale.

Basically, two things happened. First, the law was passed in October of 1986, but they made it retroactive back to January 1 of that year. That meant every sale that had been financed since the first of the year was taxed on the full sales price (meaning they were treated like cash sales). This required us to pay taxes on money that we had not yet received, which was completely devastating for our business. Secondly, it prevented us from buying and developing any new land because we couldn't afford to keep paying taxes on all the gains up front. This would not have been a problem if we had been receiving cash on all our sales—but keep in mind we were financing about 95% of our customers. This tax reform bill put a lot of our competitors into bankruptcy. Meanwhile, we were already putting out so many fires that we didn't even grasp the impact of the bill until years later. We just knew the timing couldn't have been worse.

I felt like a man selling suits, only I'd run out of suits to sell. Once we'd foreclosed the lots that people had defaulted on, then resold those, we couldn't buy new inventory because of the new law.

# THE LADIES BEHIND THE SCENES

*"None of us are as smart as all of us."*
Ken Blanchard

**TWO PEOPLE WHO PLAYED A** huge part in our survival during this time were my mother-in-law, Alma, and my wife, Paula. Dr. Robert Schiller wrote a book called "Tough Times Don't Last but Tough People Do!" Alma and Paula define this title. Their prayers, and the prayers of others, got us through the difficult times.

Alma was always so key. She would call farmers and get them to agree to work with us when we didn't have the money to make the payments that we owed them. God would give her great ideas, and Paul and I would put them into action. She once received what I call a "download" from God. On that day, God said to her, "Just dance in advance." In other words, go ahead and rejoice, because God has already provided for us.

The day-to-day operations of our business were quite a bit of work. Payments had to be collected and posted, contracts had to be typed, deeds and mortgages had to be filed, and we had to constantly make sure any overdraft fees at the banks were covered. Between the loans we had and our checking accounts, we were dealing with eight or more banks. Grandpa Lloyd would take deposits to all the banks, and the money usually had to be deposited before 2:00 p.m. Alma and Paula took care of all the paperwork and details that were required to make sure everything was in order. Keep in mind, this is mostly pre-computer days, so things were handwritten or typed on typewriters. With several hundred property owners, this proved to be fairly labor intensive for two people. My sister-in-law, Tammy, would also help them when they needed her. When you add in the stress of the financial hardships we were experiencing, it was all a lot. When tough times hit you in business, you better get the details right—especially if you work in real estate! Paul and I know that Alma and Paula's attention to detail—along with their encouragement, direction, prayers, and hearing from God—were vital for us to keep getting up every day and giving it our best.

## IT'S GETTING TOUGH!

Paul and I continued to communicate with the president of the bank and his EVP in Edmond. Once the shopping center was completed, we had $43,000 more in accrued interest on the construction loan due to the bank. The income from our leases could barely pay the insurance and overhead, and very little went toward interest. We thought we could borrow against the seven acres that was paid for to catch up on the past-due interest, but then we ran into another roadblock. We learned that both of our partners had taken out loans *against* those seven acres (without our knowledge) totaling $100,000. Then the bank our partner had previously worked for was shut down by the FDIC. Now the property was tied up in court with the FDIC and the bankruptcy proceedings of our two partners. (I'll go into more detail on this later.)

Because the Woodward Savings and Loan had gone under, we were now dealing with the bank in Edmond and the Federal Asset Disposition Association (FADA). As Savings and Loans started to go under across the nation, the Federal Savings and Loan Insurance Corporation (FSLIC)—their equivalent of the FDIC— crumbled. FADA was then set up by the government as a subsidiary of the FSLIC, for the sole purpose of liquidating and disposing of the assets from failed Savings and Loans that were acquired by FSLIC. Later, FADA turned into the Resolution Trust Corporation (RTC). On January 30, 1987, Paul and I met with Bruce F. Harris of FADA and the Edmond bank. After the meeting, Mr. Harris ordered a new appraisal and used the same certified appraiser we had used at the beginning of the loan. The property had gone from being valued at $915,000 to $318,000—ouch! As FADA started liquidating assets and selling land for pennies on the dollar, the market fell that much.

In June 1987, we received a letter from the bank in Edmond stating that to extend our loan, we would need to fill out a 100-page asset hearing document. Otherwise, they would call our note due and payable! Paul and I set an appointment, met with the bankers, and proposed a deal to strengthen the project so it would have a much better cash flow. This deal would hinge on us buying out FADA at a discount. We would put up one of our land projects that had equity as additional collateral. The bank sent two loan officers to our home office, and together we went over all the land files.

Meanwhile, we updated our financial status, which the bank sent to FADA as well. FADA finally responded in September of 1987. They stated that they would settle their portion of the loan for $85,000. The bank called and said they had some options available, so we set a time to meet. When Paul and I got there, the only options they gave us were foreclosure or to deed back the property by what's called "a deed in lieu of foreclosure." If we deeded the property back, we would be required to sign a promissory note for $250,000 each and put up additional collateral. This was not an option, so Paul countered and asked if they would discount their portion of the loan to the appraised value of $318,000. For FADA's portion of the loan, he asked if they would allow us to sign a promissory note for the discounted amount of $85,000. That note would be set up over a two-year period with monthly interest-only payments. In lending, this is what is called an "interest only loan." They said they would see what they could get us approved for.

We were actively trying to get the property refinanced. We took the proposal to another bank on Friday, October 16, 1987. The lender said it looked good and that he would let us know on Monday. But then, on Monday, October 19, the stock market crashed. Paul and I went to the bank to see if the loan had been approved. The banker we saw the previous Friday said "I can't even look at the loan. We have people panicking over the market. They're trying to pull out their money even though it's insured!"

We kept trying. But the doors were closing fast.

## MR. FAULKENBERRY
## OCTOBER 1987

Bart, Paul, and I were partners on a subdivision called Pecan acres. We bought this 160-acre tract from Mrs. Peck, who lived in Tulsa. This subdivision was in Bart's name, and the payments were annual at $30,000 per year. With the current economic conditions, sales had been very slow on all our subdivisions. Plus we were in trouble with the shopping center, and we were a couple of months out from the due date of Mrs. Peck's payment. It looked like we were not going to be able to make the payment.

One day, as I was driving through this subdivision, I started praying and asking God for help. I heard a song on the Christian radio station playing. It was Carman's song "The Champion." This song is about a boxing match between Jesus and the Devil, but he's describing Christ's crucifixion and resurrection. Hearing it, I felt incredibly inspired. I knew God would take care of us. We just needed to trust.

We'd been selling the acreages in this subdivision for $4,000-$5,000 per acre, but we were willing to drop the price for a cash sale. We received a call from a man named Mr. Faulkenberry one day, who was looking for 15 acres to build a house on. He was retiring and wanted a new home to start the next stage of his life in. He had cash, but he also wanted a deal. We toured him, and when the dust settled, he bought 15 acres for $30,000.

This would allow us to close and make our payment on time to Mrs. Peck. We were in our land office about to close, and I noticed that Mr. Faulkenberry had a worried look on his face. He sat down and told me that two days prior, when the stock market crashed, he'd lost about 50% of his retirement account. I could tell he was unsure about closing, and I felt a pit in my stomach. He finished talking, then looked at me and said, "What do you think, Jackie?"

I said, "Mr. Faulkenberry, I don't know what to tell you. I show up every day, and I used to read the local newspaper. There were so many negative things going on that by the time noon rolled around,

I couldn't pull my head up off my desk. So, I quit reading the paper." I reached over and picked up my bible, which was always on my desk, and said, "I started reading this."

I didn't say anything else. It got real quiet for a few moments. Finally, he looked at me and said, "You're right. I'm buying the land."

Whew! We closed on the land, and I thanked him. Then I walked over to First State Bank of Jones, where Kenneth Hayes was the president and escrow agent for Mrs. Peck's payment. I said, "Kenneth, here's the payment for Mrs. Peck."

"Where did this come from?" he asked.

I just smiled and said, "It was a miracle." I turned around, walked back to the office, and went back to work! Another Red Sea miracle!

## SEVEN ACRES OF COMMERCIAL LAND

Our seven acres of paid-for-land ended up having $100,000 borrowed against it because of our two partners. When we originally bought the 13 acres, title was taken in each of our names individually. When we started the shopping center project, we deeded the four acres it was built on into the Limited Partnership. However, we'd forgotten to move the remaining land over into the partnership. Since the property was still in our personal names, our partners had borrowed on their undivided one-fourth interests, which is legal. This was another lesson learned: The land should have been put in another partnership for a future project and set up where all partners had to agree on what happened. We learned the hard way.

When Paul and I realized this had happened, we found out we could borrow as well. But no bank wanted to lend on a third or fourth mortgage position. If a bank had loaned us money and we defaulted, they would have had to buy out the $100,000 first and second mortgages ahead of them. By this time in Oklahoma, property values had fallen drastically. With a $100,000 mortgage against it, this property was now underwater. We took the property to court for a partition by sale. A partition by sale, or forced sale, allows a co-owner of property to force the sale of the entire property despite the unwillingness of any co-owner.

The property had to be appraised first, which took time. This resulted in the property not selling at court (since there was more owed on it than the property was currently worth). The bank that held the mortgage defaulted and was taken over by the FDIC. So, we had interest in a property that we basically couldn't do anything with.

But God had a plan for later. Romans 8:28 says, "And we know all things work together for the good to them that love God, to them that are called to his purpose."

While at the land office one day, I received a call from an insurance company in Florida. The man on the phone said good morning and told me his name, that he was with a large insurance company, and it looked like we were partners on a property in Jones. I asked, "Where is this property?"

He said, "It's seven acres of commercial land. We thought you would want to buy us out."

I said, "Sir, have you ever been to Jones, Oklahoma?"

"No," he said.

"Well, right now I'm putting out so many fires, it's gotten to the point where I'm not able to rub two pennies together!" Then, after a second, I said, "Why don't *you* buy *us* out?"

"Well, you and Mr. Howard are 51% partners and we're 49%."

I said, "Nice try—we're 50/50 partners. And you know, I was sitting here this morning working on my mindset, and your news has just put me over the top!"

"What do you mean?" he asked.

"Well, I'm feeling much better now that I know my father-in-law and I are partners with a large insurance company."

He didn't have anything more to say after that. We said our goodbyes and hung up. I never heard back from him. His insurance company had bought a batch of notes that had gone bad that the FDIC held, which they'd probably paid pennies on the dollar for. All they had done was bought the lender's position. If they had foreclosed on it, they would have owned 50% and Paul and I would have still had our 50%. They never started the foreclosure process, and their statute of limitations ran out, so in time they lost their interest in this property. One of our partners had quit claimed his interest to us. The other partner hadn't yet, so he was still in title.

At this same time, we were also behind on the property taxes and in danger of losing the property for delinquent taxes. We were able to bring Paul's sister in as a partner (in exchange for her bringing the money to catch up on back taxes, interest, and penalties). What a lifesaver that was! We just didn't have the money right then. Thankfully, we were able to keep this tract, and we knew that at some point in the future we'd be able to sell it. So, we shelfed the property and moved on.

A few years ago, God told me it was time to get the title to the seven acres straightened out. We had a title company bring the abstract to date. The original mortgages had expired, and the insurance company no longer held an interest in the property. We needed to get quit claim deeds signed from the two partners and their spouses. The ex-banker partner was in Tulsa, while his ex-wife was still in Norman. My father-in-law got the ex-wife to sign off. She knew her interest was gone because of the bankruptcy in the late 1980s.

We then headed to Tulsa. When the old partner answered the door, my father-in-law said, "I'm Paul Howard." The man looked scared. Paul put out his hand to greet him, and a look of relief came over him. He invited us inside. He explained to his new wife that they both needed to sign this document to clear the title for us, and that he'd lost his interest in this property many years ago. I felt sorry for him, but he seemed happy, and it was good for him to see that we held no bitterness towards either partner. Like I said—when your whole world is falling apart, you just do your best.

With the other partner, even though he'd signed a deed back years ago, the title company required another deed signed. He gladly signed, and he knew Paul and I held no grudges. Ephesians 4:32 says, "And be ye kind one to another, tenderhearted, forgiving one another, even as God for Christ's sake hath forgiven you."

In 2004, with the title now clean, we could sell. The economy had rebounded, and prices were rising. I got a call one day at my bank office from my old banker friend, Kenneth Hayes. We chatted briefly and he said, "Jackie, I want to buy the corner lot you and Paul still have. I'd like to build a new bank."

He was referring to the commercial land on the corner across from the shopping center. I told him, "Kenneth, you know better than anybody there is a lot of blood, sweat, and tears in that property, so it will be pricey."

"Jackie, I know," he said. "I've seen you go through all of this."

I told him the price, and he called back and said it was a little out of their budget. He asked about the seven acres instead. We negotiated a price of $160,000 for that land and closed 30 days later. They also bought out Grady Delling's two acres and a two-acre tract that Bart owned. Today, those 11 acres are home to a beautiful bank. The bank also donated some of the excess land to the city of Jones, and they have a new library established there as well. The experience taught me much about patience, forgiveness, kindness, and doing your best. I also learned that trusting in God is a must. As the scripture says, "All things work together for the good!"

## 1986-1987 RECAP

To recap here a little: In the fall of 1986, the bill was approved through the Oklahoma Legislature to move mobile homes over to the Oklahoma county assessors' tax rolls. The Tax Reform Bill of

1986 was passed in October of 1986, our partners on the shopping center were out due to their financial hardships, and the economy took a huge nosedive in Oklahoma. In August of 1987, there were major layoffs at the General Motors plant. The stock market crashed on October 19, 1987, and people were losing their jobs and leaving the state for better economies. I vividly remember one lender saying during this time, "Oklahoma is red flagged. There's no new money coming into our state."

# ENCOURAGEMENT STORY: FA THARP

*"Everyone has inside of them a piece of good news. The good news is you don't know how great you can be! How much you can love! What you can accomplish! And what your potential is."*
Anne Frank

*"Because of the Lord's great love we are not consumed, for his compassions never fail. They are new every morning: great is your faithfulness."*
Lamentations 3:22-23, NIV

**ONE DAY LATE IN 1987,** FA Tharp came into the office. FA was a home builder who'd built my mom and dad's house in 1968. I knew who he was, but I'd never had the opportunity to meet him. We visited, and he asked how I was doing. I told him I show up every day, have faith, and try to do my best. Then he said, "Jackie, I've been a home builder since the 1950s. Our housing industry here in Oklahoma has always seen steady growth, right up until the late 1970s. Then prices started jumping with the oil boom and inflation. We had the oil bust, then prices started dropping. But couples are graduating from college now. This market will come back." Then he said something I'll never forget, "When you see things jumping in price quickly, watch out! I don't care if it's real estate, gold, diamonds, cattle, whatever—because if it goes up too quickly, it will come down."

I've never forgotten this analogy, and it has served me well over the years. Back when I milked cows, I remember how the pros would be in the front and the rookies would be in the back. They followed one right after the other without a thought, creating a cow trail. In life, people tend to do the same thing. I call it the herd mentality. If everyone is buying houses left and right, it might not be the best time to buy a house. It's probably a better time to sell. If you go opposite of the herd, then you will probably be okay. Looking back, I realize the only reason Mr. Tharp came into the office that day was to encourage a young entrepreneur who was just trying to survive. I'm forever grateful, because that 30-minute talk encouraged me and proved to be a pivotal point in my journey.

## RICK NEWBY'S PRAYER — A TURNING POINT

I met Rick Newby back in 1982. Bart bought insurance for his Jeep Wagoneer from Rick and told me, "Man you've got to meet this guy." So, I went and met Rick, and I liked him immediately.

Rick was a Farmers Insurance Agent working for his stepdad in Choctaw, Oklahoma. A friendship began between us. I watched Rick turn his life around and start serving Christ. Rick finally got his own Farmers agency.

Like me, he'd started with nothing. He'd racked up a lot of debt too from starting his own agency. When the economy started tanking and people were losing their jobs, Rick started losing customers, which hurt his business. Rick would call to give me a scripture of encouragement, and there were days God would give me a scripture to encourage him with. I remember how much his calls helped me, and he's shared with me that the times I called lifted his spirits as well. When it seems like the whole world is falling apart, it's very important to have a friend willing to go through war with you. That's Rick!

I usually went to his office in Nicoma Park, where we would have lunch. But one day, in 1987, he came to our office in Jones. He walked in the door and said, "Do you have any land for sale?"

"You bet! Are you ready to buy?" I said.

"I am ready to pray!" he said. Sales were slow, and it was tough at that time.

I said, "Yes, I'm ready to pray too!" I got a contract out and laid it there on the desk. Rick and I prayed over that contract. I don't remember everything he prayed, but I do remember he said, "Lord, I see 'for sale' signs everywhere out here. I pray that Jackie and Paul's land is more appealing to the buyers that are out there. I believe their sales will increase and they will have to order more contracts." Then I thanked Rick, and he left.

Something I need to point out here: Properties were for sale everywhere, but our main competitors were the RTC. You'll recall I discussed the RTC—a government agency—in a previous chapter. We would have a five-acre tract we'd be asking $3,000 an acre for, while the RTC would have a lot right next door that they'd taken back and were fire selling for only $1,500 an acre. Talk about tough competition!

A few weeks after Rick's prayer, I called him and said, "Guess what? I went to Quickcopy today." Our sales had increased, and I'd had to order more contracts!

Not too long ago, Rick and I were talking. He said, "Do you remember that day I came to your office in Jones and prayed?"

"Do I remember?! It was a huge turning point for me! Another Red Sea miracle!"

"Man, I was having it rough and was praying for God to help me and my business. God showed me 10 businesses and said, 'If you pray for the owners of these businesses and ask me to bless them, then I will help your business turn around'!"

"Wow," I said. "You never told me that." I told him how grateful I was that we were one of the 10 businesses! Rick and I are still great friends to this day. He went on to be very successful in the Farmers Insurance world. My family are legacy customers with Farmers because we've been with them so long!

# THE FORECLOSURE

Okay, let's jump back to 1987. Things were really starting to deteriorate. As I'd mentioned before, the Edmond bank and FADA were still willing to take a discount on their portions of the loan. But we were having no luck getting financing to buy them out.

Some friends of Paul and Alma's introduced them to a young attorney, Bill, who worked for a large law firm in downtown Oklahoma City. Paul and I met with Bill the following week, and we decided to hire his firm to help us. He gave me a list of things he would need by November 30, 1987. We quickly compiled all the documents he'd requested.

On December 10, 1987, we found out that FADA wanted to foreclose, but the Edmond bank still wanted to negotiate. Bill at our law firm said the Edmond bank attorney had sent FADA the paperwork they requested, but he thought we only had about another month left to negotiate before it went to foreclosure. On January 21, 1988, we received a letter from the bank's law firm demanding payment in full of $885,767.98.

Ouch! Now what? Hang on—there's more to come!

# BANKRUPTCY – I'M NOT QUITTING

"Failure is an event, not a person. Yesterday ended
last night. Today is a brand-new day and it's yours
to use in a marvelously productive way."
Zig Ziglar

"Therefore we do not lose heart. Though outwardly we are
wasting away, yet inwardly we are being renewed day by
day. For our light and momentary troubles are achieving
for us an eternal glory that far outweighs them all."
2 Corinthians 4:16-17, NIV

**FROM JANUARY TO JULY, BILL** continued negotiating and trying to buy us more time. However, on July 28, 1988, we received a letter from him stating that we should consider reorganization by filing bankruptcy. He then sent us to one of the best bankruptcy firms in Oklahoma City. Paul and I set an appointment with Mark, an attorney at the firm there.

I remember sitting there as Mark spoke to us about the process. I felt like such a failure. I thought to myself, *How did we get here? Is this a bad dream?* Mark sent us home with a bunch of papers to fill out and bring back to his office the next day. That night, Paul, Alma, Paula, and I looked over the papers and discussed filing bankruptcy. White sitting there pondering the pros and cons, a memory came to me: Growing up, I fed the hogs and Bart milked the cows, which he did not like. One weekend, when I was 14, I did all the feeding and milking while Bart went to visit his buddy. When he got back on Sunday, I said, "I'll make a deal with you. If you feed the hogs, I'll milk the cows." So, from then on, I had the responsibility of milking the cows.

One February night, I'd milked about half the cows when a young heifer kicked the gate down, causing the cows I hadn't milked yet to get out. It was dark, cold, and wet outside. I thought to myself, *I'm done.*

I drove back to our hog farm and walked in the house. Dad was eating supper. He said, "You're done milking already?" I said, "Done as I'm going to be. I quit!" He said, "Oh really!"

But he was nice about it. He drove me back to the dairy barn and said, "Son, there's no one else to do this. We're it. The cavalry isn't coming, and the cows have to be milked." He helped me get all the cows back in the lot, and we sorted out the ones I'd already milked from the ones I'd missed. At 3:30 the next morning, I was back out milking cows. Right then and there, at the age of 14, I learned that quitting is not an option!

After thinking back on that life lesson and our family name—which the generations before me had worked so hard to build—I said, "Paul, everyone we sold land to believed in us. I don't think I could live with myself if they somehow lost because of the situation we're in. If we lose everything, that's one thing—but if *they* lose too, that just wouldn't be right. I don't want to file bankruptcy. I will show up at the land office every day. The only way I'm going to leave will be if men in suits show up and tell me I have to go."

So, we all agreed that bankruptcy was not an option for us. Paul still tells this story today, saying that night is what kept us from filing bankruptcy. I'm grateful for my childhood days. They've paid great dividends that I couldn't see at the time. I'm also grateful that God has allowed me to remember little things from my youth. Those memories provide hope and direction.

## MR. REAL ESTATE & ESTATE PLANNING

The next day, after our discussion and decision to not file bankruptcy, we felt we needed to go talk to our regular attorneys, John Morgan and Barney Taylor. Barney had dubbed John "Mr. Real Estate."

I first met John Morgan when I sold five acres to a very nice lady who'd been diagnosed with terminal cancer. She loved the setting and had bought a beautiful old home from a small community in Oklahoma called El Reno. She planned to have the existing home moved onto the five acres so she could enjoy what days she had remaining. John represented the credit union that provided the financing for her. In our deed restrictions, there was a clause that stated you couldn't move anything that had been previously built onto the land. This was in reference to moving an existing home onto a lot, not a mobile home. Mr. Morgan required all property owners to sign off on that restriction. I was able to get everyone's signatures, then I took the document to Mr. Morgan. He looked it over and said it had to be notarized. I'm a notary, so I also asked him if he could prepare the notary acknowledgment so I could notarize all the signatures.

While his assistant prepared the document, I told him about Paul and how our business was rapidly expanding. When the document was finished, I asked what I owed. He rattled off his hourly rate, but then he told me, "Oh, forget it. There's no charge." I asked if he would be our council and he said yes. The blessing of meeting "Mr. Real Estate" would become very valuable. God used John and Barney to provide us with sound legal wisdom through many of the tough storms we faced.

Barney Taylor was also a great real estate attorney. Paul and I had visited with Barney about the bankruptcy after we had been advised by Bill, our attorney representing us in the shopping center negotiating, and by Mark, the bankruptcy attorney. At a prior meeting with Bill, I told him a deficiency judgment filed against us would cloud the title on all our available acreage inventory. (A deficiency judgment is an unsecured money judgment against a borrower whose mortgage foreclosure sale did not produce sufficient funds to pay the underlying promissory note—or loan—in full.) Bill argued with me, saying it would not affect our acreage inventory. The land is how Paul and I survived, and I knew a judgment from this project would completely shut us down.

Back to our meeting with Barney. He said: "Gentlemen, we are going to do some estate planning. We are going to move all the acreage over into corporations. That way you can still sell and repay your existing debt to the banks and farmers." (Remember, LLCs were not available yet.) Barney continued, "There is a law called fraudulent conveyance, which is an attempt to avoid debt by transferring money to another person or company. That's not what we're doing, we are just doing some estate planning, and if they want to take over your debt, we'll give it to them."

Whew, what a relief it was to hear that! He also confirmed that I was right—the judgment getting ready to hit us would literally shut us completely down.

Paul already had a corporation in place, but he'd never put any assets over into it. So, we went to work. As there was such a tremendous amount of inventory, it was a huge task to get done. Paula and I had to set up a new corporation for our development too.

A few weeks later, we were served by a process server. In a foreclosure proceeding, a process server's principal job is to deliver or "serve" legal documents to a defendant or person involved in a court case. One day, I was at Paul and Alma's house when the doorbell rang. The man at the door asked if this was the Howards' residence, and then he asked my name. He said very kindly, "Oh, I need you as well." Then he handed me the legal documents of the lawsuit/foreclosure and said, "I'm so sorry." Even the guy who delivered the not-great news was kind!

The process had begun—they were foreclosing. The court then appointed a receiver (a court-appointed individual given custodial responsibility of a property that serves collateral for a loan in default). In our case, the receiver's job was to collect rents and help manage the shopping center until the bank either sold the property or got it back.

# PREPARING FOR THE STORM

*"Storms draw something out of us that calm seas don't."*
Bill Hybels

**I RECENTLY READ AN ARTICLE** called "What does it mean if you're dreaming about tornadoes?" by Claire Lampen. In the article, Claire writes that dreaming of tornadoes tends to represent worry, anxiety, and spinning out of control. She also mentioned that lots of small worries can make you dream of smaller, skinny tornadoes, while big worries are represented by larger storms and tornadoes. I kept having a recurring dream of massive tornadoes, and they were headed straight for the shopping center.

Here was our next dilemma: Bart had partnered with Paul and I on several of our land projects, but not on the shopping center. I sat down with Bart the day after we'd visited Barney and developed our plan of action. I explained that the shopping center would be "fire sold" and that there was a huge deficiency judgment about to hit Paul, Alma, Paula, and myself. I told Bart I didn't want him to lose his equity in the joint properties he owned. It was an emotional meeting. I poured my heart out and told Bart I was sorry this was happening, and we both cried.

After trading out our interests in the different developments, here's where we landed: Bart had a full subdivision on his own, Paul was equally traded out, and I owed Bart $15,600 to buy him out of our Sleepy Meadows subdivision. I told him I didn't know if I could borrow the money, so I prayed for God's favor.

I went to Kenneth Hayes at First State Bank of Jones and applied for the loan. The next day, he walked over to the land office and asked me, "Jackie, are they foreclosing on you and Paul?"

"Yes, sir," I said.

"Okay. Give me a week and I'll let you know," he said.

One week later he came back to the office and said, "Jackie, the loan committee doesn't want to do this loan. But I've known you since you were a little boy. I'm going to loan you the money." I said, "Kenneth, I promise you I will pay the bank back."

And guess what? We did pay the loan back, and he never even required a financial statement or tax return from me. He loaned the money to me based on straight character. Amazing. Another Red Sea miracle!

# THE LADY TAKES HER CHECK BACK

*"Your setback is just a setup for your comeback."*
Steve Harvey

*"That the trial of your faith, being much more precious than of gold that perisheth, though it be tried with fire, might be found unto praise and honor and glory at the appearing of Jesus Christ."*
1 Peter 1:7, KJV

**THE ECONOMY KEPT DROPPING, BUT** our bills and obligations weren't going anywhere. Bart was now out on his own after we'd traded and I'd bought him out. Meanwhile, Paul and I kept putting out fires. Our system went as follows: When we financed a lot, we split up to 20% of the purchase price as our commissions, then the monthly mortgage payments would go towards the loan debt. If it was a cash sale, we split up to 20% of the total sales price, and the remainder went to pay back the banks and farmers. We worked on a straight commission basis, which we dubbed "chicken today and feathers the next," meaning some weeks your sales are through the roof and some weeks they are sparse!

One afternoon, I sold a lady an acre of land. She gave me $1,400 for the down payment, meaning Paul and I would get $700 a piece. I remember how broke I was and how many bills I needed to pay. I put her down payment check in my desk drawer and went home for the evening.

At 8:00 a.m. the next day, my phone rang. The lady who'd bought the land said she needed to talk to me. I met her at the office, and she said, "Jackie, I'm so sorry, but I need my money back." This had happened before in my years of selling: sometimes the customer had second thoughts. I asked her why, and she said, "My sister gave me some land." I opened the desk drawer and handed her the check back. How do you say no to free land versus paying $10,000 for an acre? Part of me wanted to be upset, but the other part of me thought: *Go ahead and thank the Lord because he has something better.*

I sat there pondering what had happened for a while. 1st Thessalonians 5:18 says, "In everything give thanks." I said, "God, where can I go but to you? You know my needs and that I have bills to pay. I thought I had a sale, and now I don't. I thank you in this situation, and I know you have something better."

One week later, a young man I knew walked into the office with his grandfather. He said, "Jackie, do you have any one-acre tracts for sale?" I said, "You bet."

We went to look at the land. And wouldn't you know, the same lot I'd given money back on was what he was interested in. We walked on the land, and he said he wanted to buy it. I took him and his grandfather back to the office, and when I asked how much of a down payment he could give, he said, "I want to pay cash!"

We negotiated, settled on $10,000, and closed in a couple of days. Here's the lesson I learned that day: It's about trust. God was seeing if I was really trusting Him or if I was leaning on my own thoughts and strength. By not being upset and getting my mindset right, I chose to obey the scripture and thank God in the situation. In return, He gave me something even better. Paul and I now had $1,000 a piece to pay bills, while the remaining $8,000 went to pay down our debt on that subdivision.

## WORKOUTS AND COLLECTIONS

On top of all the other things hitting our business, people were getting behind on their payments and property taxes. We spent a tremendous amount of time calling property owners and trying to collect payments. We always worked with them; most of our customers were trying, just like we were.

For the lots where the owners upped and left, we had even more work ahead. We would first have to get title work done to see if the owners had any judgments or liens filed against them. If they were fortunate enough to not have any liens, we would try to track them down and have them sign what's called a "deed-in-lieu of foreclosure." A deed-in-lieu of foreclosure is an arrangement where you voluntarily turn over ownership of your property to the lender to avoid foreclosure. This usually helps you avoid being personally liable for any amount remaining on the mortgage. Some of the lots had clouded titles with liens and judgments, and foreclosure was the only remedy to clear the title. It took about six months back then to foreclose, and it cost us money we didn't have. Keep in mind we had inventory we couldn't sell because we only had a mortgage interest, not ownership on those. In those situations, we still had to pay the property taxes—otherwise we could've lost the lot to a tax certificate, and later a tax sale. Whew!

Oftentimes I would show up at the office, pray for a positive day, and something good would happen. Usually, it was a phone call from Rick Newby or a friend from church. During this time, I would say this scripture almost daily: "This is the day which the Lord hath made; We will rejoice and be glad in it." (Psalm 118:24, KJV)

One day, I had to borrow $2,500 to make the farmer's payment on time for one of my subdivisions. I set up appointments with all the property owners who were behind on their payments to us and asked them to come in personally. I told them my financial counseling was free and that I'd be glad to go over all their finances to see if I could suggest ways to get their mortgage paid.

One customer I knew had a great, salaried job. His mobile home was paid for, so his monthly land payment of $200 was his total housing expense. He came in with his wife, who was crying, and I said, "I'm sorry, but I don't know where else you can live for $200 per month." I stayed kind and explained that I had to make my payments too. She stopped crying, and miraculously they started paying on time after that.

# THE SHOPPING CENTER SELLS AT SHERIFF'S SALE

*"It's easy to react if everything is going great!"*
Vince Gill

**THE SHOPPING CENTER WAS SOLD** at a Sheriff's Sale on December 6, 1988, for $200,300. On February 1, 1989, at 2:00 p.m., the court finalized the foreclosure. A deficiency judgment in favor of Homestead Savings and Loan Association was placed against all four of us for $926,295, minus the $200,300 sum that was received at the Sheriff's Sale, which left $725,995 plus interest at the rate of 18.25% annually from the date of the sale.

The judgment hung over our heads. We knew it could affect our business at any time. This was where we really had to trust God—because there was nowhere else to turn. One positive is that the building is still standing today, and we built it to last. It still looks nice and is a great asset to the new growth of my small hometown.

In time, the judgment expired. It never affected our credit. Hence, another Red Sea miracle!

# A FRIEND'S RESPONSE

*"A word fitly spoken is like apples of gold in pictures of silver."*
Proverbs 25:11, KJV

**ONE NIGHT, AFTER A TOUGH** day grinding it out, Paula and I were at our friends Rick and Sue Williams' house. Rick and I were out on the back porch encouraging one another. He would share some news of what was going on with him, then I would share right back. I started telling him about the collections and how tough it was getting. I'd called and knocked on a lot of doors that day to try and collect payments due on our receivables. Looking back, I'm pretty sure I did a whole lot more venting that night than he did. I vividly remember him listening intently. Then he said something profound: "Jackie, at least you have some doors to knock on." Wow! I still remember his words and how impactful they were to me that night. I said, "Rick, you're right. I'm sorry. I didn't have the right pair of glasses on."

In life, we're often not looking at things with the right pair of glasses—meaning we don't have the right perspective. Rick was essentially saying, "I'd love to trade places and have a chance to get paid." From that night forward, I looked at knocking on doors in a whole new light. This was another lesson that caused me to have more of an "attitude of gratitude" as Zig Ziglar says.

## KELLYVILLE STORIES

In 1982, Paul had a friend named John in Tulsa. John wanted to partner with Paul on a land deal, so Paul found 240 acres of land owned by FA Tharp in Kellyville, Oklahoma, and he put it under contract. John was to obtain all the financing, and Paul would be a silent partner. They ended up signing a contract to buy another 160 acres that adjoined the 240 acres. Paul then found out that John had used up his inheritance, and the banker said John had borrowed to

87

his limit. This meant Paul had to use his own financing to get the project started.

John was a minister and had been all his life. One weekend, he and Paul had several land appointments scheduled. John and his son didn't show up and never let Paul know they weren't coming. There were too many appointments for Paul to handle himself, so he had to tell people they'd need to reschedule. It was a rough day. When Paul finally talked to John later that day, he said, "A good friend came in from out of town, so we took him to play golf." This wasn't the first time this had happened with John. But it was the straw that broke the camel's back. Paul ended up buying John out of the project. Paul suddenly had to spend most of his time two hours away from home to sell this project, while Bart and I were running the office in Jones.

Fast forward to 1988. Paul's project was in trouble. The bank pulled him into a meeting with the entire bank board. Dr. Parham, who was on the board then, told Paul he'd recently toured the development. He asked Paul what he intended to do to turn it around. Paul said, "First, I think you know the state of affairs here in our economy, and we're working hard every day to turn this around. Do you want me to sign the project back? Or I can show you my plan to get you paid."

They agreed they didn't want the project back. Paul set up an appointment the following week, and we met Dr. Parham and Tom, the bank's vice president, at our land office in Kellyville. We all got into Paul's car to tour the development and show them the plan he had come up with. Paul and I were in the front seat, while Dr. Parham and Tom were in the back. We started off by inventorying each lot and telling them what we thought it could resell for. After about 30 minutes, Dr. Parham asked, "Paul, have you graded these roads since I was here three weeks ago?"

"No, I've not done anything to the roads," Paul said.

Tom started laughing, and then he said, "Dr. Parham, do you know what the difference is between today's tour and the solo tour you did?"

"What?" he said.

"There are two salesmen sitting in the front seat!" he said. We all laughed! Through Tom, we later discovered that when Dr. Parham came back to the board, he had painted an awful picture of the development. That made his comment even funnier.

Paul and I went to work. We found a building in Kellyville that had been a small western clothing store, rented it, and set up a land office. Then we started selling and turning the development around.

One day, we traded for a bus that had been converted into an RV. The man who traded it to us said, "I got the RV from a lady who showed poodles. She bought it from an evangelist." Things at this point were still stagnant. But God was faithful, and whenever we needed it most, we would make a sale.

Since we now had an RV to sell, Paul told me to run an ad in the Tulsa World newspaper. I ran the ad, and we parked it out in front of our office in Kellyville. A couple of months went by without any interest in the RV. But then one day I received a call from a man, and he said, "I'm calling about your bus for sale." I told him a few details and what we were asking for it. He said, "I want to look at it." I asked him when a good time would be and he said, "Now." I explained that we lived two hours away.

So, I picked up Paul and off we went to Kellyville! When we got to the office, the man was waiting. We introduced ourselves, invited him into the office, then chatted for a few minutes. When Paul started to tell him about the RV, he said, "You don't have to tell me anything about this bus. I used to own it!"

Paul and I couldn't believe it.

"Yes, my wife and I evangelized in this bus!" he said. "We saw so many miracles while evangelizing." He told us about times the bus would be running on fumes, and they would just barely make it to the next church. He said, "I work for a propane company now. I pulled up to the stop sign, looked over, and saw the bus for sale. I couldn't believe it!" He called his wife from a payphone across the street and said, "Honey, you're not going to believe it, but our old bus is for sale!"

Paul worked him a deal, and he bought the RV. Paul started telling him about all the things we were going through and how we didn't know whether we'd have to file bankruptcy or not. He listened intently to Paul, then said, "I heard an old preacher say one time that it didn't come to stay, it came to pass!" I thought, *This can't pass fast enough!*

Right there, we witnessed another Red Sea miracle. I've come to call those "God things," because there were simply too many to call them coincidences. What he told us that day encouraged me greatly. I've found encouragement to be like a cold glass of water when you're dying of thirst on a hot, summer day. Encouragement quenches the soul, and then something awesome happens—hope shows up!

As I'm writing this, I can see God's plan at work. There were times it seemed like it would never end. But we kept encouraging one another, and together we realized God was our strength through those difficult times. Whenever we were unsure of our next step, He would drop another miracle in our laps, and our hope would soar.

## THE LOSS OF OUR FAMILY FARM

In 1987, my dad's appendix ruptured, and he came close to dying. He was in the hospital a long while and was hit with a large hospital bill after he recovered. Dad was a self-employed real estate broker, and if he couldn't work, he couldn't generate income. It took him about six months to recover.

On top of that, he lost a lawsuit and was hit with attorney fees. His real estate sales were also impacted by the crippled economy. There were 160 acres we called the Bartlett place, which Dad had leased for years and finally had the opportunity to purchase. That debt was now weighing on him. Bobby, our baby brother, was in college. Bart and I did all we could to try and help, but we were struggling with our own debt. We basically had our hands tied.

So, Bart, Paul and I thought we would try to help Dad develop half of the Bartlett farm in hopes that it would get him out of debt and leave him 80 acres that were paid for. When Dad bought the Bartlett place, he didn't get a per-acre release clause. (A per-acre release clause allowed us to pay the farmer a certain amount per acre, and they would give a partial release on that acreage.) Dad hadn't planned on developing this farm, so he didn't get that clause in the contract. The farmer wouldn't give Dad a release, which meant we had exhausted all our options. There was a local bank involved too, and they were working with Dad the best they could.

Finally, Dad couldn't make the payments. The bank had to buy out the farmer's position because they held a second mortgage. The bank called Dad's note and foreclosed on him. Dad had leveraged our 80-acre family farm along with his personal home on the loan, and now those properties were in jeopardy as well.

When you see everything around you falling apart, it's tough to watch—especially when you don't have the means to help. The only thing I could do was pray. Two scriptures came to mind. The first was Ephesians 6:10, which says "Finally, my brethren, be strong in the Lord, and in the power of his might." The second was Ephesians 6:13-14, which says, "Wherefore take unto you the whole armour of God, that ye may be able to withstand in the evil day, and having done all, to stand. Stand, therefore!" Sometimes, all you can do in life is stand. That's the point we were at.

I remember the day Mom called and said a man had come by and told her that he had bought our family farm. It was tough, but we knew God was able to carry us through any difficulty.

Today, I work with a man named Gene Cobb. We help farmers and their heirs to sell their family farms. The emotion tied to these farms is a part of all farmers and their families, because of what we call the "blood, sweat and tears" of all the years of hard work on these farms. At closing, I always tell heirs, "I know this is bittersweet, but today you are receiving your inheritance." Or if it's the farmer and this is their retirement plan, I always tell them how all their hard work paid off. I then say, "We lost our family farm in the 1980s. Our inheritance was lost, but God's grace is sufficient."

Dad bounced back after the downfall of the 1980s. He went on to become a great thoroughbred racehorse trainer.

## EDDIE AND WILLELLA STEGER
## WALTER AND YVONNE LOPP

As I mentioned earlier, the farmers we bought from would owner-finance us for 10 years at 10% interest. All of them worked with us during those difficult years. We had to extend the terms to lower the payments, and we moved the ones set on annual payments to monthly.

Three of the farms were in mine and Paula's names. Two farms were purchased from Willella Steger and Mary Jane Orsini, who were sisters. The other farm was purchased from Walter and Yvonne Lopp. We were very blessed to have had these folks. They were the kindest and easiest to work with. Willella's husband, Eddie, was a neat guy. He would often stop by the land office on his way to the post office. He would walk in and tell me, "Jackie, the best things in life are free!" Then he'd point to a little bird sitting on a high line outside of my office. I learned much about his life, including how he'd meet Willella while being stationed here in Oklahoma during WWII. Willella and Mary Jane's dad, Wilbur Lopp, was a business owner in Jones who had purchased different farms over the years. His original farm—where his girls grew up—was just north of the farm my Grandma Listen grew up on. By the time Wilber died, he had accumulated several farms. Willella and Mary Jane ended up selling all of them. They carried the notes, which helped them spread their tax liability out over a few years. When we made our final payment to them, Willella said, "Jackie, you and your father-in-law are the only ones that paid us. Everyone else filed for bankruptcy."

Walter and Yvonne Lopp were also kind and fantastic to work with. They had both gone to school with my mom and dad. Walter's farm was just southeast of Jones. I will forever be grateful to these folks.

Looking back now, I see how God used these great people to help us work through a very difficult time. The only thing we weren't allowed to try to pay back was the shopping center. When the FDIC and FSLIC (which later became FADA and then the RTC) came to Oklahoma, they came to liquidate. I know and believe that if they had worked with us and others in this great state, then a lot of people would not have been forced into bankruptcy.

One survival tip we used was that if we owed someone money, we would always sit down and communicate where we were financially. If I owed the bank a small note, I would tell them when I expected to have the payment. If I came up short, I'd let them know. Communication is always vital, but it goes to another level when things start to go south. If you're honest and communicate well, you can take comfort in knowing that you're doing your best.

## THE FDIC BUYOUT & THE MAN FROM FLORIDA

Paul had a subdivision called Olive Tree Estates. The farmer held the first mortgage on this subdivision, and a bank in Norman held the second mortgage. When the bank went under, the FDIC took over the note. At the time, the FDIC had rented an entire building in Oklahoma City. Paul and I went there every other week to try and settle the note. Paul told them he just needed it to be put on payments and we needed to be able to get partial releases when our customers paid off their notes to us. We would get close to settling, then they would turn us over to someone else. We never could get anyone with the FDIC to make a decision. (Keep in mind here, Paul was not asking them to discount the note—he just wanted them to set it on a reasonable and affordable payment plan.)

A couple of years later, I was up at Paul and Alma's house one evening when Paul got a phone call from a man in Florida. This man told Paul that he'd bought a $160,000 note from the FDIC, and now he needed to collect the $160,000. Paul said, "Partner, you've got a nice second mortgage, and I'm doing my best to keep my nose above water. So, all I can say is get in line." The man started cussing, so Paul said, "If you're going to cuss, then I'm hanging up."

The man stopped cussing, then wanted to make a deal to settle the note. He asked Paul what he could give to settle with him. Paul said, "I might be able to come up with $20,000, but it's a big might!" The man asked if Paul could come up with $25,000 instead. Paul said he would give him $20,000 then, and if the man gave him five months, he could come up with the extra $5,000. They agreed on this, and Paul and Alma managed to get the money rounded up. That's the way it was back then. This man bought notes from the FDIC for pennies on the dollar after we'd tried for well over a year to get the FDIC to work with us.

After Paul sent him the money, he and Alma received a box one day full of information, along with the paid note. This box contained all the information the FDIC had compiled on Paul and Alma, as well as information on myself and Paula, even though our names weren't even on that note. It was a strange feeling to know we'd been researched so thoroughly, but such a relief for Paul and Alma to have it resolved.

One important thing to point out: Until this note was settled, Paul and Alma didn't have a way to give any of their customers in this development a release when they paid off. Thankfully, there was only one person who'd needed a release before this note was settled, and it was the only lot that happened to have had a written letter in the file stating that the bank would release it. We have no idea how that happened. Without a doubt, this was another Red Sea miracle.

# LAND BUSINESS WINDING DOWN

**Mindset**: The established set of attitudes held by someone.
**Oxford Languages**

"Your body is not in control of your mind—your mind
is in control of your body, and your mind is stronger
than your body. Mind is certainly over matter."
Dr. Caroline Leaf

"Not only that, but we rejoice in our sufferings, knowing
that suffering produces endurance, and endurance
produces character, and character produces hope."
Romans 5:3-4, ESV

**GRANDPA LLOYD ALWAYS SAID, "THE** body goes where the mind goes. If the mind says we are going, the body has to go." I started working on my health in 2001. My dad had a blockage in an artery and had to have a stent put in. I hadn't known of any prior history of heart conditions in our family. Donald Sherman mentioned to me one day that I should go to my dad's cardiologist, Dr. Fred Lybrand in OKC, and have a routine checkup.

So I went, and Dr. Lybrand did all the tests. Afterward, he told me, "Well, you've got your dad's genetics, and you've got the bad LDL." I asked what LDL was. He replied, "If your LDL is too high, over time it can clog your arteries." I asked what I had to do, and he said, "You've got to change your diet, get skinny, and exercise."

"What if I don't want to do that?" I said.

"Then I'll have to cut into your chest in about 10 years!"

"Doc, I can do that!" I said.

So, on my way home that day, I thought about how I could jumpstart this fitness journey. When I got home, I told my wife about Dr. Lybrand's report. We had a NordicTrack ski machine that had barely been used. I decided I was going to put it out in the garage, stick an old TV in front of it, and start walking at 5 a.m. every morning. Paula said, "Go for it!"

The weight started coming off. Before I knew it, I'd gotten in shape. My son was 14 years old then and was working out at a gym called The Health Club three days a week. He invited me to come lift weights with him. One day, while at the gym, I looked over at the treadmill and wondered if I could run. I hadn't liked running in junior high or high school.

I got on the treadmill one day and ran for 15 minutes. It was tough, but I stayed with it. Finally, I got to a point where I could run three or four miles. Paul has a two-tenth-of-a-mile dirt track around a roping arena, where he used to train racehorses. My daughter's blue heeler dog, Rilie, loved to run, so I started running with her at the ranch about four days a week. One day, my daughter was watching us run. She asked, "Dad, do you ever think you could run the half marathon in Oklahoma City?" I was 49 years old at the time. I thought, *Hah! No way!*

But in December 2010, I was in an accountability group with two friends, and we were setting our goals for 2011. When it got to the physical aspect, I said, "Gentlemen, I'm going to run the half marathon at the OKC Memorial!" They both looked at me and said, "If you write this down, you've got to do it!" I said, "Yes, and you two are going to hold me accountable!"

I also got them to commit to running the 5K race. When I walked out of that meeting, I thought, *How am I going to do this?*

I Googled and found a plan I could use called "Half Marathon Rookie." It was a 10-week plan, but I customized it to fit the five months I had leading up to the race. I started training, and I gave myself a goal: to cross the finish line in two hours or less. I ran four days a week, with my longest mileage days on Saturdays.

One night, I was at The Health Club, where I lifted weights. A gentleman I knew asked if I would play racquetball with him. He told me that he was training for the OKC full marathon and had run the half marathon the previous year. During a break in play, I told him I was training for my first half and then asked him for any advice.

He explained that the key is to run your own race. As men, we tend to be competitive. He told me I'd have all sorts of people pass me on race day, and it could really mess with me mentally. He said I had to learn to run my own race at my own pace. That was a tremendous help for me at that point in my race prep. I was still a bit nervous and unsure leading up to race day, but as my training got further along, I felt confident I could do this. I especially remember the Saturday I ran 12 miles for the first time. I knew that if I could do 12, I could do 13.1!

On May 1, 2011, I crossed the finish line with a time of 1:51:39. Words cannot describe how I felt. At one point during the race, I experienced what Dr. Carolyn Leaf calls, "the mind overtaking the body." My calf started to cramp about 12 miles in. I said, "Straighten up! We're crossing the finish line!" Just like that, the cramp went away!

This story is important to me because running is about endurance, and my life has been a test of endurance. The scripture in Romans 5:3-4 tells us to rejoice, because suffering produces endurance. We suffered in the late 1980s all the way to the early 1990s. Because the new tax law did not allow us to buy more land inventory, my income dwindled tremendously. I had to work on my mindset every day. A scripture I would repeat quite often was Psalms 118:24: "This is the day the Lord has made, and we will rejoice and be glad in it." This scripture taught me that no matter what was going on around me, or what my circumstances might be, I could be glad and rejoice in the Lord! When I looked up the definition of mindset and saw that it's an "established set of attitudes we hold," I realized that during those hard times, my family just kept enduring. We weren't the only ones going through hard times. I can now see how God's plan worked all along. As the Romans scripture goes on to say, "Endurance produces character, and character produces hope!"

The land business was dying down, and I knew I had to diversify my career. I enjoyed working with my family—I didn't want to leave and start over. But God's plan for my life had another chapter. I told Paul and Alma that it looked like I was going to have to find something different to do. They gave me their blessing, and we all started to pray for the next thing.

## FARMERS AGENT, THEN THE BANK

My good friend Rick Newby encouraged me to talk to his district manager to see if I might be a good fit for Farmers Insurance. I went and visited with Jimmy Wallace. He said they were looking for new agents and that he would let me know. A short while later, Jimmy called me and said, "Jackie, we want to hire you and let Rick Newby work with you in his agency until you're able to start your own agency."

Now I had an opportunity to start making some money. This was late 1991, and I was struggling to make ends meet. But God is faithful and always on time! Right when I needed it most, I'd witness another miracle.

I'm reminded of another incredible story from this time. Bart sold 15 acres of land to a couple, Duke and Sandy. Over the years, Duke would come in, visit, and share with us how God had turned his life around. He had a pallet company in OKC that his dad had started many years earlier. During the hard times in the late '80s, Duke was struggling to make his payments. We had managed to get his mortgage released from the bank, so his payments were helping us pay our bills. One day when Duke was in my office, he asked me to pray for him. He had always advertised in the yellow pages, the cost of which was around $11,000 a year. He said, "I can't afford to pay this. I'm just going to trust God." About two weeks later, he stopped in the office and said, "Jackie, guess what just happened? A man walked into my office today. He's with Wilson Food Company in packing town. They just signed a $250,000 contract with me!" We thanked God for answering this prayer. Now he could make his payments on time. Yet another Red Sea miracle!

All these stories—these miracles—reminded me of the story in the Bible where God had the ravens feed Elijah daily. We had experienced the same thing. During our financial drought, God provided for us over and over. I heard a man preach one time about faith. He said, "Faith is like reaching out and grabbing a hold of nothing until it turns into something!"

Now I had a new adventure, but there was one problem. I couldn't find peace with this new position I'd taken. I had weighed it out, and I knew that with Rick and God's help I could make it work—but I just couldn't find peace. Here I was: broke, and with a great friend who'd helped me get this opportunity. But I was miserable in my spirit.

I knew what I had to do. I called Rick and said, "Rick, God is not releasing me, and I'm troubled in my spirit." Rick is a great friend. He said, "Jackie, you have to have peace, and if this isn't a fit, call Jimmy and just tell him. He's a Christian. He'll understand." I called Jimmy and explained how I felt. Like Rick, he was very understanding.

# THE BANK

*"Change starts with you, but it doesn't start until YOU do!"*
Tom Ziglar

**NOW WHAT? WE KEPT PRAYING** and believing.

One day, I was at McClain County National Bank in Purcell, Oklahoma. I worked with one of their vice presidents, Bonnie McCall, on development loans we had with them. She had mentioned a subdivision they had taken back east of Norman in an area called Little Axe. It was 320 acres divided into one-acre tracts. There were over three miles of gravel roads, and the development had its own water system. Bonnie mentioned they had over 100 lots to sell, and that there were major problems out there. They didn't know what they were going to do. The economy was still stagnant and slow. I said, "Bonnie, Paul and I are available." She said, "Let me see what I can get done. We would love to have you and Paul sell this for us." They really didn't want to contract out the sales—they just wanted to hire someone as an employee to sell everything for them.

Paul went and talked to Bonnie. He said, "Jackie can come work for you if you want to hire him." Bonnie went to work, and they decided to bring me in to talk to me. I met with the officers and owners of the bank. Perry Nemecek was the head of lending. He said, "Jack, we want to hire you, but we want you to go out and look the subdivision over and bring us back a plan of how many hours you'll work. We value your opinion on what the selling turnaround time will be."

So, I went to assess the land. It was rough. Before he'd lost it, the developer they'd taken it back from was letting anybody move in there. He had sold some genuinely nice people in the beginning who took good care of their properties, but then there were others who didn't care. I had never seen so many car shells, so many lots littered with trash and junk. I knew the key to revitalization was getting the homeowners association reestablished. I had been told that at the last homeowners meeting, the sheriff had to come out because people were so angry. I'd also learned in real estate about the life cycle of a neighborhood. The life cycle of a neighborhood is always in one of these phases: growth, stability, decline, or renewal. We were definitely in major decline, but I saw the potential!

Suddenly, I felt a sense of peace. I knew that was where God wanted me to be!

## SETTING UP THE OFFICE

I started with the bank on June 12, 1992. My office was a used mobile home that the bank had bought from one of the employees before setting up on a corner lot in the development. When I got out there, it was set up on blocks with no electricity running to the trailer, no skirting, no porches on it, and no furniture inside. It was difficult to even get up and into the door. I went to Perry and asked him how he wanted me to proceed. He handed me the bank's credit card and told me there was extra office furniture at another of our locations. I went to work, and it took me a few weeks to get everything set up.

From the very beginning, I knew God had placed me at this project, so I prayed for Him to help and protect me. The first few weeks, every personality known to man showed up. Many were very negative and were anxious to share with me. I would listen briefly, but then tell them, "I'm sorry, but this train is rolling forward. The bank has this land now, and we are committed to doing our part." One thing I've learned over the years is that if you don't participate in a PLOM party, then no one else shows up. Zig Ziglar describes PLOM disease as "poor little ole me!" After my positive responses to the negativity, they quit coming in.

A lot of the existing property owners were angry with the former developer and anxious to tell me about it. I gave them all the same response, "We plan to turn this around and make it a great place to live once again." The developer's office was just down the street, and I never once said a word about him. I was there to represent the bank and to sell land.

My very first week, the only remaining officer of the property owner's association called and said that someone had broken into the water tower and stolen the pumps. Right then, I realized the first objective would be to reestablish the property owner's association. We set up our first meeting and sent out letters to all the existing owners. We had around 70 people at that first meeting.

At the meeting, Perry Nemecek put me in the driver's seat. He said, "Jack is here to sell the land. And since we own one-third of the property now, we want to contribute our part. We plan to have this sold out in five years or less." That night, we elected new officers and offered our sales office to meet once per month. With my previous experience with other homeowners' associations, I knew this was a major key in turning the subdivision around. I also knew I could teach them parliamentary procedures for conducting their meetings, which I'd learned in FFA (Future Farmers of America). That night, I sold five lots to existing property owners who wanted to own lots that were next to them. We were starting to build some momentum!

Steve Sherman, who is now currently the president of the bank, worked with me on all the sales and closings. I would sell the property and Steve would drive out and conduct the closing. A lot of people worked hard to help this project succeed, and I am grateful for all of them. We had a great team!

## OKLAHOMA NATURAL GAS

I was told that at one point, Oklahoma Natural Gas had considered bringing gas into the subdivision. I called them, and they had me speak to a man named Vance Stanley. Vance said, "Let me come out and look." He came out, I gave him a tour, and then I explained what we were doing. He said, "Let me go back and see if our research and engineering department thinks it's ready."

One week later, Vance called me and said, "Jackie, we need to see another 40-50 lots sell, then we might be interested." He was probably thinking, *I'll never hear from this Jackie fella again.* I thanked him and went to work.

Around six to eight months later, I called Vance and said, "Vance, I've sold the number of lots necessary for you to come back out and take another look." He came out, and he said, "Jackie, this doesn't even look like the same place." New mobile homes were moving in, and the roads had been graded with new gravel. When we got back to the office, Vance said, "Man, what an amazing turnaround. So, the cost of this will be around $200,000. ONG will look at it one of two ways. The first is that the property owners pay the $200,000 for us to install. The second is we pay for the installation within the subdivision, and the property owner just pays for the gas connection from their home to the line on the road."

I said, "Well, they don't have the $200,000, so let's go with option two." He thanked me and said he would be in touch. Two weeks later, he called me back and said, "Jackie, good news—ONG will be running new gas lines into the subdivision!" I thanked him, and when I hung up the phone, I thanked God, for I knew His favor was upon us. Paul had always said to me, "Jackie, when something good happens, always give thanks and give God the credit." James 1:17 says: "Every gift God freely gives us is good and perfect."

## WORKING MYSELF OUT OF A JOB

The bank ended up taking back a substantial amount of OREO (Other Real Estate Owned). By 1996, I had sold most of the land and properties that the bank had taken back. Besides the subdivision I'd originally been hired to sell, there were others in the same area that the bank was forced to take over along with many other properties we sold. I had basically worked myself out of a job.

One day, Don Sherman, our CEO, asked me to come to his office. Don said, "Jackie, we want to hang on to you. We have an officer position opening up. Our agriculture lender, Frank Conway, is retiring.

We would like you to take his position and be a vice president, with an emphasis on agriculture lending." Honored as I was, I asked for a day or so to think it over.

This was a big step—totally different from what I thought God's plan for my life might be. I talked to Paula, and she wasn't sure. I always laugh because Paula said, "You just don't look like a banker." I'm not sure what her vision of a banker was, but it wasn't me! After much prayer, I said, "Paula, I feel God wants me to do this." As always, she supported me. I told Don I had made my decision and wanted to talk with him and the executive committee again. In the meeting, I told them I felt God wanted me to do this. I said, "I'm not a suit and tie guy." Don laughed because—back then—everyone in the bank wore ties.

Don said, "Jackie, you always look crisp, and I'm okay with that." He went on to say, "But there are times when we may need a picture, or we attend a certain banking function, and it might be required." I replied, "I can do that."

I was suddenly a lender. And while I had tons of business experience, I needed further banking knowledge. They sent me to two banking schools at Oklahoma State University, hosted by the Oklahoma Bankers Association. These schools were a tremendous help for me to understand how a bank operates.

## MY LENDING EXPERIENCE

I'll never forget one little funny thing that happened after I moved to lending. Doyle McElwain was our evaluator. He handled cattle and equipment inspections for the bank's loans. He came into my office one morning and said, "Jack, there's one thing you'll have to avoid now that you're a loan officer."

"What's that?"

"The Velcro Syndrome," he said. "All loan officers have a piece of Velcro attached to them, so they can never get out of their chair!"

We both laughed! Several months later, he caught me in the office and said, "Jack, you are never in your office." I said, "It's your fault!" and he said, "How?"

"Because you told me all loan officers had the same problem! I'm doing my best to beat the Velcro Syndrome." We laughed and he shook his head at me.

## BUILDING RELATIONSHIPS

In 1996, my son Jed joined the local 4-H club in Noble. My brothers had been working on him since he was little about showing pigs. I knew what doing chores and showing pigs had taught me, so Paula and I agreed for Jed to have some show pigs of his own.

We got involved with the 4-H and FFA programs at Noble. We started building relationships and, in a few years, I began getting new customers from Noble who were driving to the bank in Purcell. One thing I've learned over the years is that most people in agriculture are very loyal. I feel loyalty has been lost in a lot of ways today. To me, it's refreshing to see loyalty! The bank has always been very supportive of the 4-H and FFA kids in the various communities they serve. I still auctioneer at some of the local 4-H and FFA livestock shows to help raise money to support these programs. When I was in Class IX of the Oklahoma Agricultural Leadership Program, every CEO or president of the different agriculture programs would tell our group, "Give me a young person with 4-H or FFA in their background, and they become a top candidate." They knew if a candidate had come from one of those two programs, that they had learned responsibility, leadership, speech, record keeping, parliamentary procedure, and more. I'm a product of these programs, and I can't agree enough. They teach amazing, lifelong skills to young people.

## BUILDING ME A BANK

Steve Sherman, who is now the president of McClain bank, had suggested to the executive board that he thought they needed to build a new branch in Noble and send me to manage it. One day, Don Sherman called me into his office and said, "Jackie, we're going to build you a bank to run in Noble. Go find us a location." So, we started looking.

We had some friends who owned a building on Main Street in Noble. It was a flower and gift shop that also rented tuxedos. One day, Paula and my son were in there to rent a tux for his senior banquet. The owner, Susan, told Paula that in the past week two separate banks had approached them about buying their facility. Their building had at one time been a small Savings and Loan in the 1980s that had closed. Paula said, "McClain Bank and Jackie are looking for a new location in Noble." Susan replied, "Oh, we'd much rather have Jackie here!"

Susan called me and told me that two other banks had called her. I said, "Let me talk to our ownership." When I told them about it, they said, "Let's go today." We went to look at the facility. Though we knew the existing building was too small, we loved the location. The bank owners told Susan that they would pay the asking price. There were two lots next to the location with a rental home on them. I said, "We are going to need these two properties to make this work." Percy, Susan's husband, said, "Ivan Goodman owns those properties. I'm not sure he'll sell."

Percy had Ivan's number, so I said a prayer and called. His wife Betty answered the phone. I told her who I was and why I was calling, and she said, "Well, it's our anniversary today and Ivan promised to mow the yard for me, so he's on the mower." I said, "Don't get him off the mower on my part. Here's my number—he can call when he has time." When he called later that day, I told him we were purchasing the property next door and asked if he would be willing to sell his lots. He said, "My property is not for sale, but if you want to price it, go ahead." Then he hung up. By then, I was thinking, *We're in trouble.*

But again, God had a plan. Ivan had worked for the University of Oklahoma for many years before getting into real estate. Fred Haxel worked with us at the bank, and his dad had worked with Ivan at OU. We asked Fred to negotiate with Ivan. Fred and Ivan worked a deal, and just like that we had the property! Now we just needed to build a nice building.

Ivan knew we were coming, so he bought the property just north of the bank and built a new eight-bay commercial strip building. He asked one day what color brick and trim we were going with for our new branch, because he wanted it to match. Today, there are two great looking buildings in Noble. And over time, Ivan became my great friend.

I've been blessed all my life to have nice, older men tell me their stories, and Ivan was no exception. He would come in every week for a cup of coffee, tell me his awesome life stories, and collectively we would try to solve the world's problems! Ivan's in heaven now, and I miss my friend—but I will always cherish our friendship and the great visits we had at the bank.

With the new building completed, we opened the branch in March of 2007 with a staff of seven, including myself, Margie Keely, and Eric Vickers. Margie and I had started working together in 1996, back when I was promoted to VP and she was promoted to loan assistant. Margie had over 20 years' worth of skills in the food industry, and with my years in real estate sales, we were a great team focused on excellent customer service. I had requested to have Margie come with me to the new Noble branch, but I didn't know if the request would be approved. One day, Don Sherman called Margie into his office and told her to go join the Noble Chamber of Commerce. She would be coming with me, and I knew with the additions of her and Eric, we were setting up a successful team.

Through Zig Ziglar, I learned that the best way to answer the phone is by saying, "It's a great day at _____." I liked that, so I told my staff that we would answer the phone, "It's a great day at McClain Bank." Most of the employees were young and fought me over it at first, but soon they were answering the phone this way on autopilot.

One Monday morning, an employee named Sarah said, "Jackie, I have to tell you what happened over the weekend. I answered our home phone and said, 'It's a great day!'" I said, "Sarah, it can be a great day at home too!" We both laughed! Looking back, this was one of the best things we did for customer service. A gentleman once called and said, "Is it really a great day?" I said "Yes, try missing one!" He laughed and thought that was great. Our goal was to make people feel comfortable and to be personable.

When I was a little boy—around four or five years old—Dad would take Bart and I with him to Jones. Ray Taylor had a gas station, and he would always give me and Bart a piece of bubble gum or a coke. One time, he gave us both a 50-cent piece. I've never forgotten how it made me feel as a child. So, when I first became a loan officer, I tried putting myself in the shoes of the kids coming into the bank. I know they were thinking, "What is this place?" Anytime one of my customers had a small child with them, I would ask them if the child could have a Tootsie Pop. I had a glass cowboy boot on my desk full of them. Their parents would let them pick one out, then I'd look at the child and say, "If it's okay with your mom and dad, you can have a Tootsie Pop anytime you come into the bank. If you just stand at my door, even if I have customers, we'll pause and let you get your Tootsie Pop."

Some days, I would have a customer and look up to see a little kid at my door. I would tell my customer, "These are my little buddies" and explain what the deal was. The customers loved watching them come in.

One of my little buddies was named Paige. She was two years old when her and her older brother first came in to get a Tootsie Pop. When she got a little bigger, she'd come in and get her Tootsie Pop and then give me a hug. One day, my glass boot was low, so I got the box out of my credenza to refill it, and she saw it. From then on, she and her brother got their Tootsie Pops straight from the big box! Another day, I was volunteering at the annual Noble Rose Rock Festival when along came Paige and her dad. I was manning the moon bounce. Paige said "Hi" and then went into the moon bounce. Her dad said, "I can't drive by the bank without Paige saying, 'My buddy's there!' She even knows what car you drive!"

Those kids all grew up, and they've since told me how special they felt knowing they could come into my office for a Tootsie Pop. It made them feel comfortable and unafraid. We accomplished our goal of providing a warm, happy atmosphere. People told us quite often how much they enjoyed coming into the bank.

Starting a new branch is not easy. We were the fourth bank that came to town. Dale Horton, the local agriculture education teacher, was in the bank one day when we first opened, and he said, "I was at the coffee shop, and all the old timers there were saying they didn't know why we needed four banks in our little town! I told them, 'If you ole codgers hadn't been hoarding all this money over the years, then we wouldn't need four banks!' They all laughed!"

With the help of the community, our bank's great reputation, and a lot of hard work, the branch started to grow. As I mentioned in the introduction, I met Robert Elder and helped him with a large loan on rental properties. Robert started referring investors from Oklahoma City to me, and the branch really started thriving.

McClain Bank Noble, OK branch that Jackie managed

## MY BANKING DAYS ARE WINDING DOWN

I have to be honest. When I went to work for the bank in June of 1992, I never dreamed I would end up managing a bank. I for sure never dreamed I would spend 27.5 years in banking, but sometimes God has plans for us that we can never imagine. I'm very grateful for all my customers over the years. Many of them became like family.

In September of 2018, I was praying in my home office one morning. God was really impressing on my heart that it was time to leave the bank and return to my entrepreneurial ways. I struggled with this. We had worked hard to get the branch to where it was. It's like the water pump story that Zig Ziglar talked about. When you start pumping an old hand water pump, it doesn't seem like there is any water down there. You pump and pump. Then you pour water in to prime the pump, and a little water starts to spew out. But you've got to stay with it. Finally, a good, steady stream starts to flow. After that, it's smooth sailing. That's the point we were at. We had worked so hard, and the water was flowing steadily. Suddenly I was considering leaving? That September morning, while praying, I looked up at my wall. On it hangs a cowboy picture given to me by my friend Margie Keely. It has the scripture Proverbs 3:5-6: "Trust in the Lord with all thine heart; and lean not unto thine own understanding. In all your ways acknowledge him, and he shall direct thy paths." It was like in the old western films where the cowboy surrenders. I just held my hands up and said, "I'll obey you, Jesus. I surrender!"

In January of 2019, when Steve Sherman, the bank president, came up to do my evaluation, I said, "Steve, God is calling me out of the bank." He was a little shocked, but the executive team knew my heart and how God has always led my life. I told him I wanted to give them a year—not because I was anything special, but so that my customers and the bank would have time to make the transition as flawless as possible.

That year (2019) went by incredibly fast. I told the bank I wasn't retiring; I was "Refiring!" I took this from Ken Blanchard and Morton Shaevitz's book "Refire! Don't Retire: Make the Rest of Your Life the

Best of Your Life." In an interview with USA Today about the book, Shaevitz said, "Refiring is the opposite of retiring. Retiring is going from; refiring is going toward." Blanchard stated, "Refire is to see each day as an opportunity for adventure and learning. The point is, life is a very special occasion. Don't miss it."

# THE BUTTERFLY EFFECT

*"You can have everything in life you want if you just
help enough other people get what they want."*
Zig Ziglar

**NEW YORK TIMES BEST-SELLING AUTHOR** Andy Andrews wrote a book
called "The Butterfly Effect." In it, he states, "Every move we make
and every action we take, matters not just for us, but for all of us ...
and for all time."

In the mid 1980s, Paul needed $250,000 to sure up our loan at McClain
County National Bank. He had plenty of what we called "receivables,"
which were owner-financed mortgages we could give the bank for
collateral. The $250,000 would give McClain County National Bank
a first mortgage position *and* it would pay off other banks we owed.

Paul went to Don Sherman, CEO of McClain County National Bank.
Don explained their position and stated that their bank board and
examiners were considering calling his note. Paul explained to Don
that if they called his note, he would be forced into bankruptcy, which
was not what he wanted. Paul then showed Don a plan that would
strengthen the bank's position, pay off the other lenders, and save
him from filing bankruptcy. Don asked Paul for 24 hours, then he
would let him know what the bank intended to do.

A very important fact here is that no banks were loaning $250,000
in new money on these types of collateral. The examiners didn't like
the collateral and were requesting that lenders get away from these
"receivable owner finance loans." At 7:30 the next morning, Don
called Paul and told him the bank had approved his request! Whew!

Now, here's why every move matters: The bank's approval on this
loan for Paul allowed Paul and me to survive and not be forced

into bankruptcy. We so appreciated what the bank had done, and we shared with everyone how they worked with us and helped us when we needed it most. Then, a few years later, I was hired by Don Sherman and spent 27.5 years at McClain. I currently still serve on the board of directors for the bank.

On the flip side, if the bank had pursued and foreclosed, chances are I would have never worked for them, and the story could have continued in the wrong direction. This story exemplifies how important *every single thing* you do is, just as Andy Andrews shows in his book. Andrews goes on to say, "There are generations yet unborn whose very lives will be shifted and shaped by the moves you make and the actions you take today, and tomorrow, and the next day and the next. Every single thing you do matters!" This was a major turning point in our business, and we were forever grateful for Don Sherman and his family. And we weren't the only ones they helped through this very difficult time.

Don passed away in 2016. He had a tremendous impact on my life. Today, I enjoy serving on the board with his son Donald Sherman, cousin Charlie Sherman, and nephew Steve Sherman.

# REFIREMENT

*"Retire? But I'm just getting refired. Believe me, I'm not going to ease up, slow up, or give up until I'm taken up."*
Zig Ziglar

**ON DECEMBER 31, 2019, AT** 5:44 p.m., my family surprised me at the bank to celebrate and take me to dinner. I was literally trying to finish a few final things. I have a picture of me and Margie Keely, who was awarded my position, as I'm handing over the keys of the bank. In it, my family is making me leave. It's the entrepreneur in me to keep working hard right to the end. As I watched the video of me leaving the bank for the last time, it made me feel good to know I left everything in the best standings I could.

Right after my refirement, I went and had lunch with Dr. Kelly Brown. Dr. Brown owns Custom Dental and is a published author of several books. I asked him for advice on writing a book, and he shared a few thoughts to help me. He told me he was reading Truett Cathy's book "Eat Mor Chikin," in which Truett writes, "If you're going to be a CEO, be a Chief Encouragement Officer." So, thanks to Dr. Kelly Brown and Truett Cathy, that's my new title. I truly enjoy encouraging those who God places in my path!

Today, as Chief Encouragement Officer, I'm living in the purpose God has called me for in this chapter of my life. I'm enjoying the transformation I'm seeing in those I'm coaching and mentoring. All these life experiences, as tough as they were to go through, have turned into valuable lessons that allow me to help others work toward discovering their purpose.

In June of 2021, I attended the 2021 Ziglar Coaches Summit. David Wright asked me if I would come on stage with him and Tom Ziglar for a live coaching session. I said, "Yes, God had already spoken to me that I would be asked." A special moment happened while on stage during the summit. Here's what Tom wrote in his newsletter a few days later leading up to that moment:

> "Kenneth O'Neal, one of our Ziglar Legacy Speakers and Coaches shared with our group on Thursday that several people he had spoken with in the past week had told him they felt dry. They described the feeling like they were emerging from a desert, thirsty, and parched - dry.
>
> That very morning another of our Ziglar Legacy Speakers, Melvin Pilay, sent me a text. Melvin has an incredible prayer ministry, and he is truly Born2Pray. In his text to me he told me he had been praying for me and God had put on his heart for me a scripture from the Bible.
>
> Here it is:
>
> 'That person is like a tree planted by streams of water, which yields its fruit in season and whose leaf does not wither-whatever they do prospers.' Psalm 1:3
>
> I shared the note from Melvin and the verse with our group and you could literally feel the life-giving water restore many in the room.
>
> If the past season has made you feel dry, just know you can sink your roots into God's love and truth, and he will restore and sustain you regardless of the desert you may be journeying across."

After Tom shared the text Melvin Pilay had sent him that morning, he looked at me and said, "Jackie's book will touch many. I believe it will be like Psalm 1:3 as well: to give life-giving water to restore those who read it."

# A PLACE CALLED THROUGH

"Those who embrace change are the ones who
will create the future, serve their people, and
solve problems in the best possible way."
Tom Ziglar,
"10 Leadership Virtues for Disruptive Times"

"Even though I walk through the darkest valley,
I will fear no evil, for you are with me."
Psalms 23:4, NIV

"When you pass through the waters, I will be with
you; and through the rivers, they shall not overwhelm
you; when you walk through fire you shall not be
burned, and the flame shall not consume you."
Isaiah 43:2, ESV

**IN 1981, WHILE DATING PAULA,** I would often stay the night after church with her grandparents. One morning after I'd stayed, I had breakfast with them. I remember her Grandmother Hazel told me that God had woken her up in the night and given her a scripture for me. It was Isaiah 43:2. She said, "God told me to tell you, Jackie, to never forget this scripture." It was so powerful in the moment that I wrote it in my Bible, and I just saw it again the other day.

One morning in 2010, while having breakfast again with Paula's grandfather, I asked him out of the blue, "Wilson, is it uphill all the way?" Without skipping a beat, he said, "All the way."

During this same time, I inherited a large loan at the bank that I didn't originate. It was creating a massive amount of stress for me—almost as much as I'd had on my shoulders in the 1980s. One day, after leaving the main bank in Purcell, I was driving to my branch in

Noble and I asked God, "What is going on?" Plain as day, I heard Him respond, "Jackie, you have to go through this. Otherwise, I cannot position you to where I'm trying to take you. There's a place called 'through.'" Immediately, the two scriptures above—Psalms 23:4 and Isaiah 43:2—came to mind.

That's the thing about this life: we all have a place called "through." Your "through" will look different than mine. We all experience life in unique ways, but at some point or another we all must go through something. The good news is that when you come through, you won't be the same person you were in the beginning. You'll be stronger and wiser because of what you've been through.

I've come to realize that everything I went through on the farm as a boy was preparing me for what I would go through in the 1980s, and everything I went through in the 1980s was preparing me for my leadership role in the bank. The sum of those moments in my life have led me to where I am today, encouraging others on their individual journeys.

My hope is that you can see the power of God working in a young boy's life. He was there for me in the beginning, and He sustained me through the ups and downs on the rollercoaster that was ahead. My hope also is that faith in God will bring you through anything life throws at you. God is no respecter of persons. If He can carry a pig and dairy farmer from Jones, Oklahoma through, He will do the same for you!

Within 24 hours of submitting the first draft of this book to my publisher, Paula received a phone call saying she'd been diagnosed with breast cancer. While we aren't privy right now to everything that will happen, we know that we will make it through. We aren't going to worry about tomorrow, because we know that God is already in our tomorrow. He's already there. We just need to make it through—this "place called through."

Printed in the USA
CPSIA information can be obtained
at www.ICGtesting.com
LVHW021959131023
760820LV00010B/1024